MARILYN MONROE:

MURDER COVER·UP

MARILYN MONROE: MURDER COVER·UP

By **Milo Speriglio**

Cover Design by Todd Waite

Ⓢ SEVILLE PUBLISHING
VAN NUYS, CALIFORNIA

Library of Congress Catalog Card No. 82-51319

ISBN 0-930990-77-3

Manufactured in the United States of America by
Anza Graphics/Starcolor Offset Printing, Inc.
Reseda, CA

SEVILLE PUBLISHING COMPANY

6740 Kester Avenue
Second Floor
Van Nuys, CA 91405
(213) 501-5200

FIRST EDITION DECEMBER, 1982

Dedication

To the memory of Marilyn Monroe, and the heritage that she left behind, and whose legend in death has outlived her fame on earth for the past twenty years.

Acknowledgments

First, to veteran newspaper reporter Al Stump, who in 1972 was with the Los Angeles *Herald-Examiner*, brought the Marilyn Monroe case to my attention, and introduced me to the man who would become my client, Robert F. Slatzer.

Second, to Bob Slatzer, Marilyn Monroe's close confidante for sixteen years; and who I worked with for over a decade, putting the pieces of this puzzle together.

Third, the staff of Nick Harris Detectives, Inc., whose board of directors, with their financial support, allowed us to conduct the longest case in their seventy-six year-old history.

Fourth, to Wilson S. Hong, who provided our photographic evidence through the years, including some pictures used in this book.

Fifth, to my editor, Larry Shaw, who had the true concept of my work, and produced the finished manuscript.

And to Salvatore Anza, President of Anza Graphics/Starcolor Offset Printing, Inc., who operated his plants around the clock in order to complete the printing of this book to meet our rigid deadline.

Although there are hundreds of others to thank, some of whom do not desire to be named, I thank them for their invaluable information and leads, and I express my warmest desires for their close and valued consideration which greatly contributed to this book.

About the Author

MILO SPERIGLIO

A twenty-three-year veteran investigator and criminologist, known worldwide, Speriglio is Director and Chief of Nick Harris Detectives, Inc., headquartered in Los Angeles, California. Since the turn of the century, this agency has solved some of the most noted crimes among their over one million assignments.

Speriglio's most publicized investigation was the mysterious death of Marilyn Monroe, which made every nation in the world take notice. He is listed in *Who's Who in America-West*, *Who's Who in American Law Enforcement* and *Who's Who in California*.

He is also the author (with S. Thomas Eubanks) of *How To Protect Your Life & Property* (Seville $8.95), one of 1982's most reviewed books. Speriglio's feature article (with Shelley Ross) in *US Magazine*, August, 1982, triggered the massive media attention of his investigation of Marilyn Monroe, spurring the current investigation into her death.

During the past two decades, Speriglio appeared frequently on local and network radio and television. His work is read about in newspapers and magazines around the world.

Speriglio is a full member of Mystery Writers of America, and is considered a respected investigative reporter among his literary peers. As a detective, he enjoys an equal reputation with law enforcement agencies around the world. In 1977 he was a candidate for Mayor of Los Angeles; The Los Angeles *Times* reported: "Speriglio has come out with the most sweeping program of the mayoral candidates to combat crime."

Foreword

By Kris Baldwin

Miss Baldwin is the Special Events Coordinator of the International Marilyn Monroe Fan Club. She was the first runner-up at the Twentieth Century-Fox Marilyn Monroe look-alike contest in New York, April 1982.

Marilyn Monroe was much more than a super movie star who died mysteriously. She is an American symbol, and her admirers span generations. In this book, Milo Speriglio tells us very intimate things about the actress, things only her closest friends knew.

I'm in contact with Marilyn's fans all over the world, and Milo has become one of their heros. I admire him because of his long dedication, and his persistent investigation into the death of Marilyn Monroe. Thanks to him, her name has been cleared, proving she did not commit suicide.

I never believed Marilyn took her own life. After reading all the evidence Milo obtained during his ten-year investigation, I'm convinced suicide was not the cause of her death. He proved she was murdered, and he explains why. Now that the world knows Marilyn Monroe was murdered, I only hope justice will be served.

Introduction

Most people around the world felt that Marilyn Monroe was a girl who had everything. Strangely enough, in her own opinion of herself, she felt that she had nothing at all. She found it astounding when she opened up a newspaper or magazine and saw her pictures and read about herself. This was the "personal" Marilyn, devoid of the heavy make-up required for the studio and public appearances, but comfortably attired in her white terry cloth bathrobe, her face washed and clean, cuddled on the carpeting of her Brentwood home, where she spent a great deal of her time alone.

During her reign as Hollywood's "Golden Girl," Marilyn Monroe was the most famous blond in the world, the sex goddess who received nearly 20,000 fan letters a week. These letters helped make her one of the most valuable "properties" in Hollywood. For in the era of the star system in those early '50s, some thirty years ago, at a time when Hollywood was far more colorful and glamorous than today, a star's popularity actually was measured by the amount of fan mail.

A team of high-powered publicists at the studio manufactured the Marilyn Monroe image and sold it around the world. It was their job to keep her photos and stories in print during the promotion of her films as well as in between pictures. So they created a myth—a common practice in those days—which today would be greeted more skeptically. It worked back in those glorious days of the "star system." The movie-going audiences liked what they read, supported her pictures by heavy attendance, and made her into the undisputed sex goddess of all time. Marilyn even surpassed Jean Harlow and all the others who preceded her as the unchallenged mistress of the silver screen.

The image of Marilyn that most men accepted was quite simple. The fan magazine stories, and other publicity wherever it was printed, painted Marilyn as the beautiful girl who lived in a small apartment, cooked her own meals, was looking for the ideal man, and spent many weekend nights sitting at home, waiting for her phone to ring, hoping it would be someone asking her for a date. Perhaps it might be the man of her dreams, the man she would eventually marry, who could take her away from the plastic of Tinsel Town so she would have the family she had always wanted.

This was far from the truth. Men from all walks of life wrote to her and many of the letters included proposals. The writers varied from college students all the way up to established businessmen, including several multi-millionaires. When Marilyn had the time, she sorted through some of the mail out of curiosity, and was amused by her popularity, which she was never quite able to accept. Basically, she always remained "Norma Jeane."

Her likes were much different from those of the stars of her time. She was not concerned with being "seen," as most of her contemporaries were. In fact, she seldom associated with other big stars, and passed up many an invitation that most actresses would readily accept.

Her absence at some of Hollywood's brightest events, although noticed and sometimes commented on by the then-powerful columnists, never bothered her in the least. The only times she went out dressed up in mink and jewelry were on special occasions dictated by the studio—important parties, some annual events, and a few of her movie premieres. When she was at a party and had had a few drinks, she felt comfortable and would engage in conversation with others, even tell jokes.

This is far from the picture painted of Marilyn as being shy and withdrawn. Her shyness, which has been a subject of so much writing, has been confused with the fact that Marilyn was basically a "loner."

After she had made her indelible imprint upon the moviegoers around the world, she felt that she could do what she wanted for the first time in her life. Her studio contract provided her with a security that she had never known before. Even so, she was vastly underpaid at the peak of her career. She received only $100,000 a picture, while at the same time Elizabeth Taylor commanded more than one million dollars.

Her personal life during the '50s was quite a contrast to the publicity. She did not live in a small apartment, nor cook her own meals. Neither was she looking for an ideal husband, for she was not about to forsake her budding career for a house with a white fence and children romping through the backyard.

Actually, she lived comfortably a large part of the time in hotel rooms, at the Bel Aire, the Beverly Hills Hotel, and even the Waldorf in New York. When she did rent apartments, they were not lavish or expansive. They were relatively small, but they filled her needs. A few times, she leased furnished houses, but she never had any interest in fixing up any of her living quarters, for she knew that all of them would only be temporary.

In the fall of 1961, when she decided that the time had

come to buy a home, she returned to her home town of Los Angeles and settled down in a place where she hoped to find peace and contentment.

Jayne Mansfield owned a big pink castle on Sunset Boulevard, while others had big homes, such as Lana Turner, Zsa Zsa Gabor, and Marian Davies. Marilyn was not attracted to that type of living. She wanted to be inconspicuous, for she had no "airs" to put on. All she was looking for was a small, Spanish-type home that would assure her of some privacy.

She found such a house at 12305 Fifth Helena Drive, off Carmelina, in Brentwood. The house was at the end of a cul-de-sac, with a high concrete wall surrounding the premises. It had a medium-sized living room, an average dining room, a master bedroom plus two smaller bedrooms, a guest house and a rundown kitchen that was badly in need of repair. There was a nice but small front yard, and in back there was a kidney-shaped swimming pool (which Marilyn never used) and a large backyard boasting a lot of plants and fruit trees.

The small one-story home, built in the 1920s, looked like that of a blue collar worker rather than an actress like Marilyn Monroe. But the purchase of this house, the only one she had ever owned, stimulated her interest in planting her roots firmly and forever in Los Angeles. Unfortunately, she did not know at the time that in less than six months from the date she purchased it, she would be found dead in her master bedroom of the Spanish house.

Milo Speriglio
Los Angeles
November, 1982

xiii

Contents

I
The Death Scene

1. INT. (NIGHT) MASTER BEDROOM

The camera OPENS on a CLOSE SHOT of a broken pane in a bedroom casement window. We see the broken pane in clear focus and the contents of the room: an open entry door to the bedroom, an open door to the bathroom off the bedroom, a few hand-woven round "cobra" baskets alongside one wall, a pile of clothes against the wall in the far background with a stack of several large purses, and a mattress and box spring in the immediate foreground, covers thrown about with a large beige comforter, the slender, motionless body of a blond female stretched out nude diagonally across the bed. CAMERA HOLDS and then pans and MOVES IN CLOSE for a good look at the many pill bottles on the nightstand beside her bed.

2. ANOTHER ANGLE: THE MASTER BEDROOM

CAMERA MOVES IN SLOWLY TO FOCUS on a bottle of pills—now empty, the bottle lying on its side but the label readable, the cap a few inches away. The lights in the room are on and we see a telephone cord running up over one side of the bed and under her, her right arm outstretched toward the phone which is on the white carpeting below her head. CAMERA HOLDS as music comes up TO A STING:

CUT TO:

3. ANOTHER ANGLE: THE BODY ON THE BED

As the CAMERA HOLDS, then moves in slowly to reveal positive identification of the subject matter, the credits start to roll:

MARILYN MONROE — MURDER COVER-UP

4. *Here we hold a FREEZE FRAME while the rest of the credits pass over the scene. Then...*

The ironic thing about what you have just read is that it is not a real movie script. Although Marilyn Monroe was the star, she was not acting. In fact, this was her last role and her final scene. The body described was her dead body, just as it looked when it was discovered on the morning of August 5, 1962. No movie producer, without vast research and personal information, could ever reconstruct that death scene nor assemble the cast of characters who played key roles in her death.

To explain why, I will go step by step, clue by clue, with an ultimate goal of unraveling the puzzle of Marilyn's death, and unveil the record of two decades of

18

investigation that reads more strangely than fiction. This is the amazing true story of the Marilyn Monroe murder cover-up.

On the morning of August 5, 1962, at exactly 4:35 a.m., Sergeant Jack Clemmons of the Los Angeles Police Department—who was the weekend Watch Commander at the West Los Angeles station—was told by a caller that Marilyn Monroe was dead. Clemmons hurriedly wrote down the name of the informant, Dr. Hyman Engelberg, and the address of the Monroe residence at 12305 Fifth Helena Drive in the Brentwood area. Quickly, Clemmons appointed another officer to take his place, and hurriedly took off toward the Monroe home.

There had been a lot of prank calls at that time, reporting deaths of famous celebrities, so Clemmons' job would be to hold back the press and crowd if it were a fake call. If it were for real, his job would be more demanding. He knew that many news reporters—and Los Angeles is filled with hundreds representing media all over the world—had car radios tuned to the police band. Either way, whatever he found, he knew there would be problems, so on his way he radioed for a second squad car to meet him at the house for assistance.

Clemmons turned off Sunset Boulevard on to Carmelina, a wide artery of a street from which more than thirty Helena Drives, all cul-de-sacs about a block long, extend like fingers every block both north and south of Sunset. Marilyn's house on Fifth Helena Drive was at the end of a cul-de-sac. Clemmons parked outside the massive wooden gates that Marilyn had had installed when she bought the one-story Spanish home just six months before, and noticed three cars filling the short driveway.

He knocked at the front door in the relative quiet of the morning, noting that he was the first outsider on the premises, and was greeted by Mrs. Eunice Murray, who identified herself as Marilyn's housekeeper-companion. Clemmons first asked her if Marilyn Monroe was really dead. Mrs. Murray confirmed that Marilyn was dead. Clemmons asked her when the body had been discovered. Mrs. Murray told him she had discovered the body shortly after midnight. Clemmons asked who else was in the house. Mrs. Murray told him that two doctors were there, Dr. Ralph Greenson, Marilyn's psychiatrist, and Dr. Hyman Engelberg, her internist. Clemmons asked how long the doctors had been there. Mrs. Murray told him they had been there since about 12:30 a.m. Then Clemmons was ushered into the house and taken to Marilyn's bedroom.

There he saw a body spread diagonally across the bed, covered with a sheet. The two doctors were in the room. Clemmons noted that one had his head in his hands, looking at the floor, while the other seemed to have a smirk on his face. Clemmons walked over to the bed, gently pulled back the sheet, and immediately established that the dead body was Marilyn Monroe.

In death, she looked very much unlike the sexy blond goddess he had seen sing and dance her way across the wide screen. Her face was minus any make-up. She was lying face-down, and the whole front of her body from head to toes (the anterior) was flushed with a deep purple coloring. The veteran detective knew that lividity, or the settling of blood, had taken place over a period of many hours (in a dead person, whatever the position at death, the blood always seeks the lowest level, turning that portion from ashen gray to dark purple, depending on how long the body has remained either undiscovered or unreported). Also, the body was extremely rigid, which indicated that rigor mortis had set in several hours before. Both of these cursory observations confirmed Clemmons' belief that Marilyn Monroe's last breath had been taken about eight hours before—sometime between

8:00 and 9:00 p.m. the previous night of Saturday, August 4, 1962.

Clemmons then asked the two doctors why they had taken so long in notifying the police. One doctor, according to Clemmons, just shrugged his shoulders, while the other remarked that they "were just talking." About what? Clemmons asked. Neither doctor offered an answer.

Clemmons examined the room and found that it was in perfect order. It was not the kind of room a victim of an overdose of sleeping capsules would be found in, for in those severe cases—and in his profession he was knowledgeable of many—the victim most always goes into convulsions. It is a painful death, contrary to those who think it is an easy way out. In those last minutes the victim gasps for air, vomits all over, falls down over furniture, even breaks things.

None of this was evident, yet the doctors suggested to Clemmons that of the fifteen bottles of over-the-counter and prescription medicines that were on Marilyn's nightstand, a bottle labeled Nembutal was empty. Dr. Engelberg told Clemmons that he had ordered a prescription refill of this drug (Prescription #20853 from the Vicente Pharmacy) just two days before, and it had contained fifty capsules.

Clemmons noticed that Marilyn's housekeeper-companion was walking in and out of the various rooms as if she were walking on eggs. He also noticed that she was clearing out the refrigerator, throwing out everything, and that the washing machine and dryer were running full blast. Just what would she be washing at a time like this? When he asked Mrs. Murray why she was cleaning things up so much, she replied, according to Clemmons, that she realized that the house would soon be sealed by the coroner's office and police, and she wanted to make sure that everything was clean. Clemmons

21

thought that this was a decidedly unusual action.

But the oddest discrepancy Clemmons noticed was the lack of a drinking glass. If Marilyn had taken four dozen Nembutal capsules, where was a drinking glass, a bottle of some kind, a coffee cup, any type of receptacle that would hold liquid? He searched, but there was none to be found. He wondered just how Marilyn could have swallowed all of those sleeping capsules without the aid of any liquid. He also wondered how the doctors surmised that Marilyn swallowed those sleeping capsules. How could they be so sure, when he knew full well that only an autopsy would reveal the real cause of death?

It was about this time that Clemmons decided things just weren't "kosher," and he felt the doctors were lying to him. He also knew that even though Marilyn possibly had been taking Nembutal for sleeping purposes over a period of time, those individuals who do take these pills are quite aware of the amount that they can consume, depending upon their tolerance. As he thought about it, more doubts poured through his mind as to whether or not Marilyn Monroe really had committed suicide.

On weekends, the Los Angeles County Coroner's office assigns local coroner's representatives to work in the outlying areas of the city that is larger in number of square miles than any other in the United States. Each month, under a rotation system, a different mortuary is used, since the downtown coroner's office has less than fifty percent of its normal working personnel and has to depend upon help from the assigned representatives. Westwood Memorial Cemetery was the representative for the month of August 1962. So it was that Guy Hockett, one of the owners of the mortuary, received the call in the early hours of the morning to pick up Marilyn's corpse.

Hockett and his son Don were literally stunned when they received the news. They found that the house was secured behind the outside gates from members of the news media, neighbors, and curious onlookers. Using a nondescript white van, they entered the residence driveway and backed up to an entrance several yards away from the front door.

Meanwhile, Sergeant Jack Clemmons was going off duty, and the case was turned over to Sergeant R. E. Byron, who came in and took over the investigation. Clemmons' last duty that morning was to call his friend James Dougherty, a fellow poice officer in Van Nuys, who had been Marilyn's first husband, and break the sad news.

Hockett ordered everyone out of the bedroom and made the customary inspection of the room, assembling the pill bottles in an effort to help the coroner's office. Hockett stated that although he had been told Marilyn had been dead for about three hours, he could not believe that at all. Both he and his son, after they had completed their work, were convinced by the much-advanced state of rigor mortis that Marilyn had to have been dead for over eight hours, if not more, by the time they strapped her stiff body to a gurney wrapped in a blue blanket and loaded it into their truck. Then they sped away to their mortuary, where Marilyn's body was placed on an embalming table, awaiting the notification of her next-of-kin before they could embalm her remains.

Both Guy Hockett and Sergeant Clemmons, acting independent of each other, knew that Marilyn had been dead since about 8:00 p.m. Saturday night, August 4, 1962.

The time factor was the first indication that somebody was lying.

It was the first sign of a cover-up.

II
Case File 72-4813

In was another smoggy day in the City of the Angels in September 1972, when a newspaper friend of mine by the name of Al Stump, an investigative reporter for the Los Angeles *Herald Examiner*, called me at my office at Nick Harris Detectives, Inc. He told me a story that was hard to swallow.

"Marilyn Monroe was murdered, I'm not kidding you one bit," Stump concluded. He went on to say that a recent news item reported that Bob Slatzer, also a friend of his, had received threats on his life. Slatzer had written a manuscript about the life and death of Marilyn, and he did not believe she had committed suicide. "He needs your help, Milo," Stump said.

I was stunned. My imagination overflowed with curiosity. I had heard many tall tales before. Stump advised me that Statzer had know Marilyn Monroe for some sixteen years. "He checks out in my book. Talk to him yourself," Stump suggested. I agreed to meet them in mid-afternoon.

Slatzer had better have some hard facts, evidence and documentation, I thought to myself as I waited for them to arrive. When my secretary notified me that they were waiting in the reception area, I stood up from my desk, straightened my shirt, pushed a few files aside, and went to meet them. I saw Al's familiar face, and with him was the man who would eventually put me on the track of our longest-running case.

Stump introduced me to Robert Slatzer, who carried a thick briefcase, and we talked for a while. Slatzer was knowledgeable about Marilyn, quite articulate, and dressed conservatively.

"Mr. Slatzer, just why do you think Marilyn Monroe was murdered?" I asked. For the next three hours he gave me reason after reason, and supported them with considerable documentation. Now I was spellbound by his story, and almost convinced Marilyn had not taken her own life.

Stump remained quiet during the whole session, just listening to what Slatzer had told him once before, and puffing away on his pipe. Slatzer excused himself and went to the men's room. I asked Stump, "What do you really think about all this?"

"I believe he is on to something big, Milo."

I still had some doubts, and hoped this was not a hoax. "Something I have to do," I said, and went to our research division and requested a fast background check on Slatzer. When I returned, I confronted Slatzer. "Have you ever been polygraphed before?"

"No, why?" he snapped back.

"I want you to take one, just to satisfy my own mind," I told Slatzer. I explained that polygraph is not just a lie detector, but is also a truth detector. Slatzer agreed to be examined.

Soon the background check arrived on my desk:

CONFIDENTIAL REPORT ON ROBERT SLATZER
Born April 4, 1927, in Marion, Ohio. College graduate. Newspaper reporter on Eastern and Midwestern newspapers.

He was the author of short stories and paperback novels. Wrote, directed and produced some action-adventure movies in the 1960s. Was an independent writer-director-producer at Columbia Pictures.

The report went on to mention he was married to a nurse in 1954, and to a model in 1960. Both marriages ended in divorce, and he had no children. Our in-house microfilm records showed no criminal court records.

One thing that Slatzer had mentioned was not found in the report. That was his claim of once being married (for five days) to Marilyn Monroe. That would become my key question for the polygraph.

Using a voice-stress polygraph unit, I asked some minor questions to set his voice pattern. Then I shot him the loaded question. "Were you once married to the film star, Marilyn Monroe?" He responded in the positive, and the polygraph showed he was truthful.

After the test, I asked Slatzer if he could furnish any proof. He said the original marriage license had been destroyed, but offered me the identity of a witness.

His witness was Noble Chissell, who later told me he had been the best man at the wedding. Slatzer and Monroe had been married in Mexico on August 4, 1952 (exactly ten years before she died), and had spent their wedding night at the Rosarita Beach Hotel. I ran a background on Chissell, and he too was quite credible.

Slatzer told me up front that he could not afford the services of a professional private investigator. During the first ten years after Marilyn's death, he had conducted his own investigation, using his own funds. Slatzer agreed to pay part of the expenses, and the board of directors of the agency, which I chaired, agreed to pay the investigation cost. At that time we did not expect that the "crime of the century" would take us ten years to solve. The case was assigned a low priority, since we had no paying client, and it was worked between regular assignments.

III
The World Takes Notice

"Marilyn Monroe was murdered," I declared in a worldwide press conference. Little did I realize that this would be perpetuated in the media for months afterwards, nor did I conceive that I would force the low-key Central Intelligence Agency to "vehemently deny" that they did kill Marilyn Monroe.

This is how it actually started, and what really was said, and later was distorted in the news. It all began in August 1981, one year before the twentieth anniversary of Marilyn's death. Shelley Ross, then a producer of the Tom Snyder "Tomorrow Show" for NBC called and wanted to send me to New York to appear on TV to discuss Marilyn's untimely death. Because of prior commitments, I had to decline.

Nearly a year passed, and once again Miss Ross called my office. "Milo, I have an assignment from *US Magazine* to do a feature story on Marilyn. The twentieth anniversary of her death is coming up, and I'd like to talk with you."

After we met in my office, and Shelley suggested that we collaborate, I felt I should do so because I owed her one.

29

The five-page story titled "Who Killed Marilyn Monroe?" carried my by-line with that of Shelley Ross.

This lead article prompted reporters all over the world to call for interviews. I granted as many of those as time permitted. During the first week I spent twelve to fourteen hours a day responding to questions from the media and I was exhausted, primarily because for a lot of the broadcasts I made around-the-world there was a time difference, and I found myself talking at all hours of the day and night from Los Angeles, to places like Australia or deep into Europe.

I decided to hold a news conference on August 4, 1982, at the Greater Los Angeles Press Club, in hopes of ending this media blitz. I had advance releases printed and circulated, advising that I would answer all questions at 9:00 a.m. that morning. I did not plan the timing; the *US Magazine* article had hit the stands, and the interest continued to build until the anniversary of Marilyn's death.

Before the conference, a news reporter with the Los Angeles *Herald Examiner*, Robert Knowles, phoned and said that he was writing a piece on Los Angeles County Coroner Dr. Thomas Noguchi, who he referred to as the "Coroner to the Stars," and asked if I would give him a few quotes about the coroner who performed the autopsy on Marilyn. I agreed.

During this brief interview, Knowles inquired as to what I might say at the news conference. I discussed a few of the items, and thought no more about our conversation. The next morning I was handed a copy of the newspaper and saw that I made the front page. The headline read:

BIG REWARD OFFERED FOR
MARILYN'S LOST DIARY

My quotes about Dr. Noguchi evidently never made this edition. However, Knowles had done a pretty good job of reporting, ferreting out some of the information that the rest of the press had to wait for until my news conference.

Like a bolt of lightning, the wire services picked up the story from the *Herald Examiner*, and I found myself inundated with calls from the press wanting to know more about the red diary. I declined to discuss any of the important topics that I had planned the following day at the news conference, and I would only talk about the diary since the news had already been leaked out. The missing diary became one of the most important major news stories of the day.

I arrived at the Greater Los Angeles Press Club about 8:15 a.m. that morning to discover that a great number of the media were also there setting up their cameras. Phone calls from the press all over the world, wanting to beat the wire services, were coming in for advance information. I counted nine television cameras, representing all the networks, cable news, and Los Angeles channels. In addition, the wire services, the photographers and an estimated eighty-five reporters were present. This would be one of the most covered news events in Los Angeles history.

The red diary, in my opinion, had received so much prior media notice that I hardly mentioned it at the press conference. Yet the volume still continued to receive extensive coverage. I made a very strong statement when I declared, "After a decade of investigation, I conclude Marilyn Monroe was murdered."

"By who?" a reporter asked.

"Perhaps a dissident-type faction, like a C.I.A. type group," I replied, adding, "may have been included in the cover-up."

"C.I.A.?" somebody from the media responded.

I looked over, disregarding that remark, and continued to mention some of the reasons I had come to the conclusion that Marilyn Monroe was murdered. My final declaration in my opening statement was that I *demanded* an official investigation into the death of Marilyn Monroe.

Much to my surprise, soon afterwards this demand was granted. I was surprised to pick up the newspaper and find the story that Mike Antonovich, a member of the Los Angeles County Board of Supervisors, had recommended to the other four members of the board that the investigation into the death of Marilyn Monroe should be opened and reviewed by the office of the Los Angeles County District Attorney. Just two hours later that morning, after the announcement was made by Antonovich in a 9:00 a.m. meeting, the Board of Supervisors in a unanimous vote requested that the Los Angeles County District Attorney, John Van de Kamp, open the Marilyn Monroe case for investigation.

Although John Van de Kamp agreed to do so, and made a formal statement to that effect, he did not call it a reopening of the case, but referred to it as a "review." However, if it is only a "review," they are certainly doing a very thorough probe which in my opinion should merit the title of a major investigation.

In the meantime, on August 4 and the next day, in newspapers all over the world, front page stories proclaimed: "CIA KILLED MARILYN, DETECTIVE CLAIMS." The strange thing about this is the fact that I never made such a statement. I phoned both the Associated Press and United Press International. They did not misquote me, I was told, but sometimes a quote will be shortened. That was fine, but my statement now was totally out of context. The media had played up just this small part, and there was nothing I could do about it. Even a journalist from Russia and another from China called; it was extremely difficult for me to convince them that the C.I.A. did not kill Marilyn. And this was not an impression that I would want either to leave with the C.I.A. or to give

China or Russia. I knew it would be a weapon to use in their propaganda against the United States.

Finally, I "cleared the air" with the C.I.A., and notified William Casey, the Director. The C.I.A. replied:

> We appreciate the fact that you have gone on record stating that the Central Intelligence Agency was not involved in Marilyn Monroe's death. Actually, the CIA had nothing to do with her death... We congratulate you on your excellent record as Director of the Nick Harris Detective Agency and encourage you to continue your good work.

The reply was nice and I appreciated it very much, but this was a letter that the public would probably never see. Still the headlines around the world continued to report that the C.I.A. had murdered Marilyn Monroe, according to my statements. Even "Entertainment Tonight," a popular syndicated network television show dealing in current personalities and situations, blasted this accusation and showed me on film at the press conference saying only, "A dissident faction of..." Again the public was influenced not by what I really said, but by what the interviewers announced.

Some of the news media suggested that I did this for publicity. Where they made their mistake in this accusation is the fact that they failed to do their own homework, because for the past twenty-three years I have been an international newsmaker. And not because of the Monroe investigation, but for major news events throughout these years. In 1981 alone, the press covered me extensively: *Newsweek, Business Week, People Magazine, Money Magazine, TV Guide* and many other magazines, feature newspaper articles, wire service stories, local and network radio and television, including "ABC Night Line", "In Search Of", "20/20" and others too numerous to mention.

33

The news accounts, however, did not present my evidence, and did not follow me on my ten-year investigation into Marilyn Monroe's mysterious death. They only played upon a few of the facts I reported, none really in detail, and often not as I actually disclosed them. What follows will be a true account of this intensified investigation, not only in my probe, but the initial investigation started after the death of Marilyn Monroe by my client, Bob Slatzer.

IV
The Death Theories

Although it is a matter of record that Marilyn Monroe's body was discovered the morning of August 5, 1962, and her death is listed as of that date, the real time of her death has been estimated by knowledgeable people to be approximately 8:00 to 8:30 the night of August 4, 1962. In both Bob Slatzer's investigation at the time of her death, and my follow-up ten years later, that fact remains true.

Jack Clemmons, the police sergeant who was the first authority to arrive on the death scene, stated that Marilyn had been dead for at least eight hours, as evidenced by the intense discoloration of her body and the rigor mortis. This meant that she had been dead for more than the "three hours" asserted to Clemmons by her doctors, Greenson and Engelberg.

According to Clemmons' original statement, when he first arrived at the death bedroom at approximately 4:40 a.m. in response to the call that had come into the West Los Angeles Division of the L.A.P.D. at 4:35 a.m., he was told by the two doctors that Marilyn had been dead for approximately three hours.

When Clemmons examined the body of the deceased, Marilyn Monroe had been dead for at least eight hours. This is fully corroborated by Guy Hockett, principal owner of Westwood Memorial Park Cemetery, the coroner's representative who took her body to their mortuary at dawn on the morning of August 5, 1962. Had Marilyn been dead for only three hours, according to the statements given Clemmons by the doctors, then I must presume that when they arrived at the house at approximately 12:30 a.m., Marilyn Monroe was still alive.

This further adds to the discrepancies in the statements given to Clemmons, who made a record of these "times"—and instantly knew that such a schedule was difficult to believe.

Guy Hockett and his son Don, who removed the body, also said that Marilyn had been dead for "at least eight hours"—so who were the doctors trying to fool?

This is further corroborated by Hockett's statement that Marilyn's body was "stiff" and had to be "bended properly" to fit on the gurney covered with the blue blanket that they strapped down and took out to their vehicle.

It might also be of interest to the reader that most reports state Marilyn's body was taken out of her "front door" of her home, which is not the case. Instead, it was taken from her master bedroom, down through her living room, and out through the French doors to the waiting van to be driven off to Westwood. The news film on file clearly shows that her body was taken out of the rear part of the house through the living room double doors facing the swimming pool, and loaded into the vehicle, which had pulled up to an open area between the garage and the guest house, which was not attached to the main part of the house at the time.

As a point of interest, the house as it is now has the garage and guest house connecting. That was not the case in 1962. At that time, there was a space between approximately seven feet in width, which was then a garden where Marilyn had planted "herbs" the housekeeper would use in omelets for Marilyn's meals. After Marilyn died, her house was sold at auction to Dr. Gilbert Nunez (who died a few years later), and the garage was expanded from the old one-car type into a double garage connecting the guest house to the main part of the structure.

I point this out mainly because most of the stories that have surfaced through the years have stated that her body was brought out through the front door of her home, which is strictly erroneous.

After Marilyn's body had been placed in the van, it swept out through the main gates of her home, making several diversionary sweeps on various streets to enable the Hocketts to lose the pursuing press.

The real cause of Marilyn's death is only one of the obscure elements in the case.

In September 1962, Robert Slatzer had carefully put together and analyzed the circumstances of Marilyn's death. The inevitable deduction was obvious not only to him, but to other members of the media—including Florabel Muir, Walter Winchell and Dorothy Kilgallen, to name a few. To circumvent a coroner's inquest—which there should have been on this case—Dr. Theodore Curphey, then Coroner of Los Angeles County, appointed a "Suicide Investigation Team" to investigate the circumstances of the death of Marilyn Monroe. This consisted of two doctors from the Los Angeles Suicide Prevention Bureau, who were to question "those persons who were close to Marilyn in the last days before her death." It was, by the way, their "first" assignment.

I learned that those persons questioned, whose names were not to be disclosed, included her two doctors, the housekeeper, her press secretary Pat Newcomb (who admitted this to Slatzer), and the handyman, Norman

Jeffries II, a nephew of the housekeeper. From this so-called "psychological evaluation" that ensued, Marilyn was depicted as "suicidal, ...giving up hope, having tried suicide on numerous occasions, ...not willing to live and go forward, and [in] other depressive moods." Our investigation of those persons around Marilyn Monroe at the time of her death showed this was completely hogwash.

First of all, the team did not investigate and talk with those persons who were the "nearest and closest" to Marilyn before her death. These included my client Bob Slatzer, Allan "Whitey" Snyder, her make-up man of sixteen years, and his wife Marge. Other persons close to her and who would give truthful answers as to Marilyn's last days, were not questioned.

In my own investigation, I discovered that Marilyn had purchased a whole new wardrobe from Saks Fifth Avenue and Jaks of Beverly Hills, which is quite inconsistent with a person comtemplating suicide. She had told Slatzer less than twenty-four hours before she died, that she was planning to hold a news conference on Monday morning, August 6, 1962, "if Bobby Kennedy refused to answer the calls she had placed to him through the switchboard of the Justice Department in Washington, D.C., or from his location at the St. Francis Hotel in San Francisco, where he had checked in the afternoon of August 3, 1962, with his wife Ethel."

According to police reports, verified by Sergeant Jack Clemmons and the hotel desk at the St. Francis Hotel, Robert Kennedy was there. Also according to police records, Bobby Kennedy was listed as having checked into the Beverly Hills Hotel during the late hours of the night of Friday, August 3, 1962. Bobby Kennedy *was* at the Beverly Hills Hotel, had checked out about noon on August 4, 1962, and had gone to Peter Lawford's house. That is a matter of record.

According to my client, who interviewed a neighbor who was having a card party that Saturday afternoon (August 4, 1962), Bobby Kennedy was seen with a man carrying a bag that resembled a "doctor's bag," entering Marilyn's house about 5:00 p.m. that day. This was also witnessed by a few other members of her Saturday afternoon bridge game. The appearance of Bobby Kennedy at Marilyn's house did not really attract that much attention, for the lady who saw him walk down the short street of Fifth Helena Drive (the men had left their car parked out on Carmelina) said: "Look, girls, there he is *again*."

Mrs. Murray, the housekeeper-companion, denied this, but later admitted that she was not at Marilyn's home all afternoon. In fact, she had left Marilyn's house for a couple of hours, so she really could not know who came and went. This supposedly left Marilyn alone in the house with Pat Newcomb, her press secretary, who had spent the night of August 3 at Marilyn's house, and who denied in an interview with my client—the only interview she has ever given out on Marilyn—that Bobby Kennedy was there.

Yet, if we jump to the time after Marilyn's death, less than a couple of days later Newcomb was flown directly from Los Angeles to the Kennedy compound at Hyannisport, where she stayed for more than ten days before embarking on a trip to Europe. There she spent a few months and according to information on her passport, she visited about eleven European countries. I found it strange that she never would talk about it or offer an explanation.

When she returned from her European trip, she was hired by the United States government and worked in an office adjacent to that of Bobby Kennedy in Washington, D.C. It was said at the time that she packed only her suitcases, leaving behind an apartment full of other personal belongings including her furniture.

But to return to that mysterious night of August 4, Pat Newcomb had also told Slatzer that she first learned of Marilyn's death about 4:00 a.m. the morning of August 5, five minutes *before* the police were notified. She said that she received a call from Milton "Mickey" Rudin, Marilyn's attorney, who told Pat that Marilyn was dead. Pat further stated that Rudin had called her from Marilyn's house.

Bear in mind that Marilyn had scheduled an appointment with Rudin for Monday afternoon, August 6, to change her will "and get rid of a lot of leeches," as she told Slatzer. She was referring specifically to Paula Strasberg, her dramatic coach and mentor. Marilyn had fired Strasberg on Friday, August 3, and wrote her a check for a one-way airline ticket to New York. Marilyn had told Slatzer the week before that the Strasbergs, Paula and Lee, were "deep into me for a few thousands of dollars, for they were playing the stock market very heavily and losing." This makes one suspicious about Marilyn's will, which had been orchestrated by Lee Strasberg just about a year before her death, at a time when she was very sick in bed with a cold in her New York apartment at 444 East 57th Street.

It seems obvious that there was much activity in Marilyn's home from the time she *really* died until the time the police were notified at 4:35 a.m. on the morning of August 5, 1962. Further evidence is that on the morning of August 6, two well-dressed men with "Eastern accents" confiscated Marilyn's telephone records from the files of General Telephone Company in Brentwood.

Sergeant Jack Clemmons, after seeing the death scene, said, "It looked like the whole thing had been staged. She couldn't have died in that position (face down, stretched out swanlike). To me, it was an out-and-out case of murder!"

Now, if Marilyn had taken orally the contents of the bottle of Nembutal, suggested to Clemmons by one of her doctors, where was a drinking glass or any vessel with which Marilyn could have ingested all of those capsules? Clemmons found no such drinking glass in her room, which was allegedly locked and had to be broken into through a side window.

It was common knowledge among those who knew Marilyn well that she found it difficult to take even an aspirin or a capsule without the aid of liquid. Even when she did use liquid, she could take only one at a time, for she had a great fear of choking. Sometimes she would get a pill or capsule caught in her throat and spit it up. Yet the report would later come in that she "gulped down nearly fifty Nembutals in a matter of seconds." This feat would be almost impossible for an experienced sword-swallower.

The scenario had been given to the police—the empty bottle theme—the missing Nembutal—but when Dr. Thomas Noguchi performed the autopsy, he publicly stated that no such capsules were found in her digestive system. Now two county agencies were at odds with each other as to how Marilyn *really* died.

Our investigation went a little deeper, and here are the unexplained points:

1. Why did Mrs. Murray have the washer and dryer operating full blast when Clemmons arrived at the house?

2. Why was she cleaning out the kitchen, ridding the refrigerator of all perishables, explaining to Clemmons that the house would soon be sealed?

3. Why did Mrs. Murray call her handyman son-in-law, Norman Jeffries II, to come over and repair the broken window before the police were called?

4. What were the doctors *really* talking about—and why did they neglect their duty by waiting so long to call the police?

5. What were the contents of the boxes Mrs. Murray was loading into her car, which Clemmons noticed while he was proceeding with the investigation?

6. Why was Mrs. Murray, the last person to see Marilyn alive, according to the 1962 police reports, alarmed at seeing a "light" under Marilyn's bedroom door?

These are just for openers.

Before Jeffries arrived at Marilyn's house to repair the broken bedroom window, a wire service photographer, Glen Waggoner, made his way along the narrow pathway that ran past Marilyn's bedroom to the back of the house and took a few pictures. The subjects included the death bedroom *after* Marilyn's body had been removed and a finger pointing to the broken window. They were the only photos of the bedroom, although pictures were taken of Marilyn's body on the bed from various angles by police photographers. These were in the original police and coroner's files, but since then have disappeared.

Now we have the story of Marilyn's dead body being found stretched out across her bed, assumed by the police to be a victim of an overdose of barbiturates. But other theories surfaced which should not be completely discarded. Among them are the following:

1. She actually died at Peter Lawford's house just north of the Santa Monica Pier (the old L.B. Mayer beach home), where Lawford and his wife Pat (sister of the Kennedys) entertained not only John F. Kennedy but also Bobby Kennedy. The theory here is that both Lawford and Bobby Kennedy allegedly took her dead body in a car back to her house. (Yes, Bobby Kennedy was placed at Peter Lawford's house that night of August 4.)

2. Marilyn, who had made a few visits to the Cal-Neva Lodge shortly before her death, died there and her body was flown to Santa Monica Airport and driven by car to her home.

3. Perhaps she did not die in her bedroom after all. There is some strong speculation that she could have died in another part of the house, possibly the guest house. If so, her body would have had to have been carried out the

front door of the guest house, onto the walk to the main house, and through her front door, since the guest house and front door entrances were separate, non-connecting, and about fifty feet apart.

All three of these alternates are quite believable because of one important fact: there were many bruises on Marilyn's body. This meant either that she died during a struggle with an assailant before she was killed, or that she was given a hypodermic to calm her down and the dose was so lethal that it killed her. Such bruises could have been caused by the bouncing of her body in moving it to the bedroom of her home, in a sack or otherwise.

In any event, none of these theories should be discarded completely. After all, we only have the word of Mrs. Murray, the housekeeper-companion, who later revealed in her book *Marilyn: The Last Days* that she (Murray) had long experience in dealing with psychiatric patients. It was Dr. Greenson who had first touted Marilyn into hiring Mrs. Murray. At that time, Marilyn did not realize that Murray had been a longtime friend of Dr. Greenson. In fact, in 1949, Murray had sold Greenson her Spanish-style home in Santa Monica. In her book, Murray states the date to have been 1961. Wrong!

Mrs. Murray's book was written with her niece, Rose Shade. There is an interesting paragraph in Shade's Introduction to the book:

"She [Mrs. Murray] worked with many kinds of patients. Some were seriously ill with depression or schizophrenia, while others, like Marilyn Monroe, were merely recovering from stressful experiences and needed supportive aid to reestablish life along more structured lines."

Robert Slatzer disbelieved Mrs. Murray's humble position in Marilyn's household from the very beginning. To quote again from Rose Shade:

"She [Murray] was drawn to psychology, feeling a need to work with people and their problems. Eunice read and studied, and when an opportunity came to care for a psychiatric case in the patient's home, Eunice was prepared with enough knowledge and understanding to work under the guidance of a psychiatrist as his aide, helping in any kind of therapy that seemed indicated."

Yet when Slatzer interviewed Mrs. Murray, recording that interview on tape, he asked her if she had any psychiatric training, and she replied that she did not. However, when her book was published in February 1975 (Pyramid Books, New York), she stated otherwise, which theoretically could swing all of her previous statements in a 360° turn.

And what did Pat Newcomb mean when, allegedly forced to leave the house after Marilyn's body was taken away (which she denies but Mrs. Murray affirms), she said to Mrs. Murray, "If I had been here, this wouldn't have happened."

Digging a little deeper, it was discovered that it would have been impossible for Mrs. Murray to have been alarmed at seeing a "light under Marilyn's closed door." Prior to her death, Marilyn had had the house carpeted with a thick white wool carpeting from India, supplemented by a thick pad underneath. Marilyn found it difficult to open and close her door, as the nap of the white wool carpeting caused considerable friction. When she showed this to Slatzer, less than a month before she died, he told her that she would wear off the nap of her expensive carpeting with the doors, whose bottoms should be cut off so that they would close without difficulty.

To test this, Marilyn turned the lights on in her bedroom one night and closed the door. It closed so tight and the high-pile carpeting was so thick that Slatzer could not even see a light in the bedroom. Yet Mrs. Murray stated to the police—and this appeared on their original report—that it was the "light under her door" that attracted Mrs. Murray's attention to Marilyn's room.

Interestingly enough, in her book thirteen years later, Mrs. Murray said:

"I knew that the new white wool carpet filled the space under the door. The surface wool had piled up as a result of contact with the swinging door. This I remembered later, but not until I agreed that I had seen a light under the door. Such are the pitfalls of demands under pressure when accurate reporting is desired."

And:

"In retrospect, even shortly after the event, I knew that the light was on because I had gone outside and parted the curtains. I may have agreed when questioners jumped to the conclusion that I had seen the light under the door..."

Again, the "the light under the door" is on in the original police report. Mrs. Murray also told that same story to the press the next day, and it was published. Thirteen years later she gave the above altered explanations.

Additionally, when Slatzer interviewed her in 1973, eleven years after Marilyn's death, it was *not* the light under the door that originally attracted her attention, but the telephone cord of one of Marilyn's two telephones.

Again in her 1975 book, she added:

"The telephone cord led to Marilyn's bedroom, but there was no sound of conversation within..."

As time passed, it was not the light under the door—nor could it have been—but the telephone cord that Mrs. Murray had failed to mention to the police.

As Walter Winchell told Slatzer, "Strange, how stories change when they have time to think things over."

V

The Investigation

The subtle use of words, such as those used in advertising, could well be applied to the investigation of Marilyn's death and the results of her autopsy. As newsman Paul Harvey once told a group of advertising executives, "In the showroom of an automobile agency, the man who wants to buy a car takes a good look at the convertible. He even imagines speeding down the highway with his mistress beside him. But when he and his wife actually buy a car, they pick the hardtop, a combination of the standard sedan and the open convertible."

And why does a woman pay five dollars for a jar of a certain cleansing cream, when she could have bought a bar of soap for less than a dollar? The soap only promised to make her clean. The cream promised to make her beautiful.

All of this applies to the analogy I am making with reference to Dr. Theodore Curphey, the Los Angeles County Coroner in 1962, who circumvented a coroner's inquest by forming a committee of two psychiatrists, called the Suicide Prevention Bureau, to investigate the cause of Marilyn's death.

If we were able to play on words regarding subliminal

advertising in the media, the team could have well been called the "Murder Investigation Team"—but no, "Suicide Investigation Team" sounded better. "Suicide" made the public believe only one thing: Marilyn Monroe was a "suicide" and their job was to find out why she had committed that act which has been listed on her death certificate for the past twenty years.

It might be of interest to the reader that the Suicide Investigation Team *did not* exist until *after* Marilyn was found dead. In fact, she was their first subject. The ironic situation here is that they did not set out to investigate whether she had actually committed suicide, but rather *why* she had done it. The die had been cast, and the subliminal advertising of using the words "Suicide Team" led most people around the world actually to believe Marilyn took her own life.

Her death was listed as "probable suicide," and was never investigated as to whether or not that was the actual truth. "Probable suicide," as we have been told by the coroner's office, is "suicide by accident," meaning that an individual could have taken some sleeping pills on going to bed, then awakened, forgetting the previous pills, and taken more. Nevertheless, under no such circumstances would an individual—especially Marilyn Monroe—have taken four dozen Nembutals plus some chloral hydrate capsules. The obvious method, consistent with many pill-takers, would be to take just a couple more, not a whole bottle, for it has been established that most persons on sedatives know their own consumption.

None of the testimony that labeled Marilyn as "despondent" and "having the will to give up" and "had tried to commit suicide on several other occasions" was taken under oath. Therefore, not one of the persons questioned faced the possibility of perjury charges, which would have been demanded if a coroner's inquest had been made.

They did not seem to be interested, from what Slatzer and I discovered, in what went on in her home the night she died. All they seemed to be interested in was Marilyn's psychological make-up, her various moods and habits, and her personality, all of which they conveniently suggested as being the causes of her suicide.

Both Dr. Ralph Greenson and Dr. Hyman Engelberg were interviewed. Pat Newcomb told Slatzer that she had been called in to give her observations. But most curiously, Marilyn's housekeeper-companion told my client that she was never called in. Yet she was the last person to see Marilyn alive, according to all recorded information.

The final report was delivered to Coroner Theodore Curphey, who held a news conference and read off the cursory report of the Suicide Investigation Team's findings.

"On the basis of all the information obtained," he told the media, "it is our opinion that the case is a probable suicide."

But questions poured in from a curious press.

"Was Marilyn a dope addict?"

"No, not in the normal sense that we use the term addict. But she was psychologically dependent upon the drugs. Miss Monroe took drugs daily and, in the last two months of her life, was taking low to moderate doses."

"Did she take the lethal dose in one gulp or was there an interval of time involved?"

"We estimate that she took one gulp within, let's say, a period of seconds."

"Will you tell us who supplied the basis for your findings?"

"We will not expose the names of the people who gave their accounts and reports to us in confidence."

All of the above was printed in the Los Angeles *Herald Examiner*, and the statement ended as follows: "Beside her bed was an empty bottle which had contained fifty Nembutal tablets. The presumption is that Marilyn took forty-seven of them at one time."

First of all, although it could have been a slip of the tongue, Nembutals are "capsules," not tablets. And that so-called "presumption" bears looking into a little more.

Let's go back to the death scene in which Dr. Engelberg stated that he had prescribed a Nembutal prescription for Marilyn a couple of days before her death and there should have been fifty capsules in the empty bottle. That was written down on the police report and seemed to have become the "theme" of her death.

We must assume, from the team's findings, that Marilyn did take three of those Nembutals, fell asleep, awakened and took the other forty-seven capsules. However, this is not the truth, for the identification on the empty bottle Dr. Engelberg referred to reads: "Empty Container, #20858, 8-3-62, Nembutal, 1½ gr. #25."

According to respected forensic pathologists who have examined the autopsy and the "team's" statements, twenty-five Nembutals could not have raised the blood level to 4.5 mg. percent of barbiturates and 13 mg. percent of pentobarbital in her liver.

The autopsy report lists only eight vials of medicine found in Marilyn's room, when there were actually fifteen. Although some were non-prescription, according to Guy Hockett and the report made by Sergeant Byron (who took over when Clemmons went off duty), the seven vials that were not listed might have included one that contained Nembutal. It would have to have been the original vial which Marilyn had refilled on Friday, August 3, 1962. The question here was, if that vial was one of the seven not listed, was it empty or full? It is highly unlikely that it was full, for otherwise Marilyn would not have obtained a refill.

More curious is an interview that Dr. Greenson gave

Maurice Zolotow, in which said: "I didn't see the Nembutal bottle on her night table [when he found her dead and before Dr. Engelberg arrived]. I think the fight may have been because Pat Newcomb had taken the pills away..."

It reasons that if Pat had taken the Nembutals away from Marilyn, then how could she have committed suicide at all?

The reference Dr. Greenson was making in his interview with Zolotow, was to the doctor's statement that he had asked Pat Newcomb to leave that Saturday evening (August 4) because Marilyn resented the fact that Pat had taken some capsules the night before and slept twelve hours, while Marilyn had also taken some and slept only six hours.

Now, if Dr. Greenson did not see the empty bottle on the nightstand, or even in Marilyn's bedroom, as he has stated, how did it reappear by the time Sergeant Clemmons arrived on the death scene?

It was Dr. Engelberg who told Detective Clemmons that Marilyn had obviously swallowed all of the Nembutals. Yet, as we said previously in our analysis, Marilyn could not even swallow an aspirin without a glass of water or some liquid. Therefore:

1. No drinking glass was found in her room (remember that allegedly, according to Mrs. Murray, her door was locked until Dr. Greenson broke in). So *where* was the missing drinking glass if we are to presume that Marilyn swallowed all of those capsules?

2. And if Marilyn was injected with a syringe, as according to some top forensic pathologists, then what happened to the syringe?

Dr. Thomas Noguchi, in his original report, stated that Marilyn died of a heavy concentration of 4.5 mg. per cent of barbiturates in her blood—which, according to these forensic pathologists is enough to kill at least three healthy cows, or several persons.

At this time it should be explained that Nembutal is the *product name* of a drug that falls under the category of "Sedatives and Hypnotics." The generic name is pentobarbital. A blanket category further describes Nembutal as one of the members of the "barbiturate" group, a derivative from barbituric acid. Now comes a most interesting diagnosis in Dr. Noguchi's findings:

The original *Report of Chemical Analysis* was dated August 6, 1962, and signed by Chief Toxicologist, R.J. Abernathy.

A second or supplemental *Report of Chemical Analysis*, signed by Dr. Abernathy, and dated August 13, one week later, reveals that there was a higher amount of pentobarbital (Nembutal) in her liver than the week before —not 4.5 mg. per cent, but 13.0 mg. per cent. According to the supplemental report, chloral hydrate, also known as "knockout drops" in liquid form was present in 8 mg. per cent in her blood. Marilyn had chloral hydrate in capsules of green color, meaning they were the strongest available, representing 1½ grain each, or 500 mg., yet the original report stated that phenobarbital (the generic name for chloral hydrate) was "absent."

If chloral hydrate was absent, in the first report, then just *how* did it turn up in her blood a week later?

It only makes sense that Marilyn had swallowed forty-seven Nembutals, it would be quite evident in the autopsy. First of all, the company that manufactures this drug purposely has a yellow dye in the gel of the capsules which will stain the esophagus and digestive tract of a person taking them. (The street name for Nembutals is "yellowjackets.") Any person taking just one of these capsules will have the telltale dye in his system for a few days.

If Marilyn had swallowed all of those capsules, it would mean that there would be partially undissolved capsules in her stomach, and there would be traces of yellow dye in her system, meaning there would be very visible traces of these capsules in her system. But when Dr. Noguchi stated in his autopsy that he found no Nembutals, or traces of the yellow dye, it means she did not take them orally, which is the only way capsules can be ingested.

The only thing that Dr. Noguchi, according to his report, found in Marilyn's stomach was about 20 cc. (equivalent to an amount that would fill a teaspoon) of what he referred to as a "brown mucoid fluid." He further stated:

"No residue of the pills [sic] is noted. A smear made from the gastric contents and examined under the polarized microscope shows no refractile crystals."

The purpose of examing the contents of the stomach would be to show exactly what drugs were in it.

In this case the 20 cc. of mucoid fluid would be boiled in a beaker to crystals, and examined under a polarized microscope. The cautious eye of a toxicologist would tell him instantly if there were drugs in this crystalline extract. Each drug, whether it be Seconal, chloral hydrate, or Nembutal, or any other barbiturate, would have an individual and recognizable appearance—much like snowflakes, all of which have different sizes, shapes and forms. No such drugs could be found in Marilyn's digestive system.

Dr. Noguchi further states, in his tracing of the digestive system, that: "...the contents of the duodenum [the first section of the small intestine], is also examined under polarized microscope and shows no refractile crystals, meaning it was found to be empty after death."

So far, there is no evidence that Marilyn swallowed *any* capsules of any kind. All of the forensic pathologists I know of who have read Dr. Noguchi's report feel that he was remiss in not going further and tracing the duodenum into the small intestine, in search of any capsules she might have ingested. But Dr. Noguchi did not. He openly stated that he did not test that vital organ. He also stated that in 1962 they did not make tests of the small intestine because facilities in the coroner's office were not available. The autopsy report plainly states that the small intestine was saved for further toxicological study. Yet Dr. Noguchi stated in the final section of his report on the examination of Marilyn's digestive system that:

"...the remainder of the small intestine show no gross abnormality."

That one little sentence does mean one thing: there must have been some type of an examination of the small intestine. Yet Dr. Noguchi admitted this organ was *not* tested. Why?

When Slatzer conferred with Dr. Sidney Weinberg, Chief Medical Examiner of Suffolk County, New York, and one of the most distinguished forensic pathologists in his profession, there was quite a difference of opinion. He stated that it was strange, in his opinion, that the autopsy report (which he diagnosed in detail) stated that the Los Angeles Coroner's Office started to examine the small intestine, then claimed they could not do it for lack of facilities. Dr. Noguchi stated that no facilities were available to test the small intestine in 1962, yet Dr. Weinberg stated that such facilities were available then at both U.C.L.A. Medical Center and at the University of Southern California. This was also confirmed to reporter George Carpozi of the New York *Post* and author Tony Sciacca, who wrote a book in 1975 about Marilyn's strange death.

Slatzer's initial investigation proved tht the autopsy report available to the public (1962) was *not* the original report. The late Thad Brown, Chief of Detectives and a friend of Slatzer's, told him that even the police department knew that the autopsy reports had been altered, lost, changed, and reconstructed. Lionel Grandison, the deputy coroner's aide, stated that this had happened. The body diagrams, both front and back (anterior and posterior), showed bruises on Marilyn's body, but when he saw them a day later, no such bruises were shown or mentioned. The evidence had been destroyed and changed!

Going back to the late afternoon of August 4, 1962, Mrs. Murray stated to my client that Marilyn had had nothing to eat or drink that day. Yet Pat Newcomb told him Mrs. Murray had fixed sandwiches for both her and Marilyn, and that Marilyn did eat food that afternoon. If Marilyn consumed food with Pat Newcomb, as Miss Newcomb has previously stated, Marilyn's stomach would *not* be empty according to our medical sources. What happened to her food? There was too short a time for it to pass completely through her system.

Gathering the analysis of several noted forensic pathologists, the autopsy report states that Marilyn had a very high amount of barbiturates in her blood and in her liver. The toxicology lab stated that Marilyn's kidneys had been tested for barbiturates and there were none present. It Marilyn had taken those capsules, the drugs would first have been broken down in her stomach, then absorbed through the duodenum from which the blood would carry them to the liver, and then they would go back into the blood which would carry them to the kidneys as waste matter to be excreted. Here is where the autopsy report falls apart.

If the barbiturates were concentrated in the blood and liver, with no signs of them in her kidneys, this would mean that the first two steps in the process had been bypassed—and the only way to bypass the stomach and the duodenum would be by injection.

Dr. Weinberg states: "...The findings in the autospy report are certainly not characteristic of an oral ingestion of large amounts of barbiturates. One must seriously consider the possibility of an injection or the use of a suppository to account for the toxicology findings."

I have never heard of one case, in all my years as an investigator, where a suppository was used to commit suicide. And if so, where was the container of the suppository? It is just as mysterious as the lack of a drinking glass or a syringe. It adds up to one thing: regardless of how Marilyn was murdered—in any of three ways—evidence most certainly had been destroyed.

The autopsy report states that "no needle marks were found." However, claims were submitted to probate to be paid by her estate by both her doctors, Hyman Engelberg and Ralph Greenson. Dr. Engelberg put in a claim that said he gave Marilyn an injection on August 3, and also visited her home the same day (but not stating what he did). From July 30, 1962, through August 4, Dr. Greenson stated that he saw Marilyn seven times. On Thursday, August 2, he saw her twice, once at his office and once at her home. On August 4, he stated he saw Marilyn at her home. All the other visits were at his office. Neither doctor stated in their claims exactly what they gave her or what services were performed, except for the one injection by Dr. Engelberg on August 3. One thing must be remembered: Dr. Engelberg did state the dates of certain injections prior to Marilyn's death. Dr. Greenson did not, yet psychiatrists do give their patients injections.

Only one bruise remained on the chart available in 1962. It showed a bruise on the upper part of Marilyn's left hip, a place, according to Dr. Weinberg, which looked very much like an injection site.

"Either the investigation is incomplete," Dr. Weinberg stated, "or they're not telling us everything they've found."

Dr. Weinberg added: "It is extremely rare for a female to commit suicide in the nude. It can occur, but it is so unusual that one has to become suspicious of the possibility of the manner of death other than suicide. During the past twenty years in my own experience [stated in 1973] I have only seen one such case and it was by gunshot, not drugs." Dr. Weinberg added, that it is not consistent with the modesty of a female to commit suicide in the nude.

Bear in mind the following:

(a) Marilyn always wore a bra to bed when going to sleep.

(b) She also wore earplugs upon retiring.

(c) She always wore a sleeping mask.

None of the above items were found on her body, according to her housekeeper-companion.

Why did Dr. Greenson suggest that Mrs. Murray stay over that particular night with Marilyn? (She had not planned to by her own admission.)

Why did Dr. Greenson ask Pat Newcomb to leave? (Pat denies this. She said she left of her own free will.)

What was Dr. Greenson doing in the bedroom with Marilyn for over a half an hour, while Pat Newcomb and Mrs. Murray "talked" in the living room.

If Pat Newcomb left before 6:30 p.m. that night, why did Dr. Greenson answer the phone when Ralph Roberts (Marilyn's friend and masseur) called to confirm their 7:30 dinner date that night? (Dr. Greenson told Roberts, "She's out," and hung up. Normally the phones were always answered by Marilyn or Mrs. Murray.)

But getting back to the medication Marilyn had in her bedroom and which she was allegedly taking;

Nembutal: 25 capsules, 1½ grain (100 mg.) aka sodium pentobarbital.

Chloral hydrate: 10 green capsules, 7½ grain (500 mg.) aka phenobarbital.

Starting with the Nembutal, it is quite evident from our findings that Marilyn did not ingest orally any capsules which resulted in her death. However, since 4.5 mg. per cent of Nembutal was found in her blood, according to the first report, she could have gotten it only one way: by syringe. It must be remembered that in 1962, sodium pentobarbital (Nembutal) came in liquid form in vials for injection use. This is obviously the answer.

As far as the chloral hydrate capsules are concerned, let's look at a different theory to compound the one above. Prescription #20570 of fifty capsules was bought on July 25, 1962. A refill (using the same prescription number) for another fifty was purchased on July 31, 1962. When Marilyn was found dead, only ten capsules remained. Therefore, ninety capsules had been used from July 25, 1962, to (theoretically) August 4, 1962—a total of ten days.

It is not conceivable that if Marilyn had taken the usual dosage of three capsules a day for ten days, the amount left would be sixty—meaning she might have consumed thirty over that ten day period. Now, if somebody were to give her an extra six capsules a day by dumping out the powder into her milk (which she drank in addition to champagne and water), she could have been poisoned slowly. Under normal circumstances, the regular dosage she took on her own volition would have not stayed in her liver but passed through her system via her kidneys. She could not taste the chloral hydrate and the end result over that period of time would be to poison her. Then the heavy injection of Nembutal in liquid form with a syringe would carry her into dreamland forever.

This supposition should not be discounted, but taken rather seriously. It could actually happen. In ancient days, that is how some people were killed. And Marilyn did have the extremely high percentage of chloral hydrate in her liver, 13.0 mg. per cent, according to the *supplemental toxicology report*. According to forensic pathologists, it had stacked up in her system so fast that she was unable to pass it through her kidneys—she was receiving it faster than it could have been excreted.

Even the distinguished E. Forrest Chapman of Bellvue, Michigan, a man with impecable credentials, said after examining the autopsy report:

"...the findings furnish high suspicion, if not proof, that Marilyn was murdered. The total absence in the digestive tract of a barbiturate, even microscopic crystals of same, indicates a non-oral route of administration. And in the absence of a needle and syringe on the premises, the above conclusions are partially or fully warranted."

Twenty years later, on the anniversary of Marilyn's death—and not one to celebrate, but investigate—Dr. Theodore Curphey, who lives in Pasadena, completely ignores the possibility of any wrongdoing in the autopsy and investigation of the death of Marilyn Monroe. He merely shrugs it off by saying it was handled properly and the case is closed. But it it?

The Los Angeles County Board of Supervisors, spurred on by Supervisor Mike Antonovich, voted one hundred per cent to request John Van de Kamp, the Los Angeles County District Attorney, to investigate Marilyn's death as it should have been done twenty years ago. After all, the Board of Supervisors appoint the County Coroner, and have recently removed Dr. Thomas Noguchi from his office on certain charges of misconduct of his duties, which Noguchi is now fighting.

Marilyn Monroe was Noguchi's first big case which helped make him "Coroner to the Stars," as he has been labeled by most newspeople. And his first important case—that of the blond sex goddess of the silver screen, reverred throughout the world—for twenty years haunted his office to such an extent that he still has not lived down his autopsy report that is viewed by his own peers as being very questionable.

The fact, according to my investigation, is that this was a murder which they tried to make appear as a suicide, and failed.

There is no statute of limitations on murder, otherwise this case would not have been opened up for investigation two decades later. And obviously, there must be a few worried individuals out there wondering what is going to happen. Undoubtedly, they are squirming now more than they did the night Marilyn was murdered.

We know it to be a fact that Marilyn Monroe was not a suicide. The whole thing was one big cover-up, which now, twenty years later has bounced back for detailed investigation.

Even today, the autopsy alone, not to mention a few persons who were close to Marilyn, and are still living, are highly suspect.

In a press release Norman Mailer passed out for a press conference on July 18, 1973, there is an interesting statement:

"In 1962...Dr. Litman, a psychiatrist, and Dr. Norman Farberow, a psychologist, of the Suicide Prevention Center were employed to do an in-depth 'psychological autopsy' for six weeks whose results indicated that Marilyn was a perfect suicidal case."

When asked to explain the lack of residue in the stomach, Dr. Litman announced that it was "a routine fuck-up."

Years later we would learn that at the time of Marilyn's death, even the coroner's office was "fucked-up."

VI

Lionel Grandison's Confession

In the first week of October, 1978, newscaster Ridgely Allison from Los Angeles radio station KPOL, narrated a two-hour tribute to Marilyn Monroe. The program included many of Marilyn's songs from her pictures, and my client was the key guest.

Slatzer was later approached by the engineer who had recorded the show, Lionel Grandison, who had been introduced to him by Allison. Although I was invited to attend the show, and make an appearance commenting about the investigation, I was out of town and could not appear.

It turned out that Lionel Grandison at the time of Marilyn Monroe's death worked in the coroner's office as a deputy coroner's aide. After he had left that job he had decided to completely change his career and go into radio and television broadcasting. Although his name rang a bell with Slatzer, the significance of that meeting became quite interesting.

On the show, Slatzer had been making certain references to his book, of which Allison had received a copy a few years before. Grandison took the book from

Allison, who was using it as a guideline for the show, and glanced at it. It happened that Lionel Grandison's signature appeared on Marilyn Monroe's death certificate, and when he mentioned this to Slatzer, there was a whole new revelation. For Grandison was a man that Slatzer had tried to contact back when Marilyn died, but who seemed to be unavailable. The fact that he had signed Marilyn's death certificate, and had been the man who ordered her body from Westwood Memorial Cemetery downtown to the main coroner's office that Sunday morning of August 5, 1962, made him a person that my client wanted to talk with twenty years ago. Now, Grandison had surfaced, and agreed to give Slatzer an extensive interview.

The interview, which was taped in a vacant studio of KPOL radio, on the afternoon of October 28, 1978, follows: (Slatzer will be identified in this question-and-answer session as "S," while Grandison shall be identified as "G.") The taped session, which lasted approximately three hours, was transcribed, and this is a condensation. It should be considered quite serious "inside information" as to what happened in the coroner's office when Marilyn Monroe's body was brought in for examination.

> S. Back in 1962 what was your official position at the Los Angeles County Coroner's office?
> G. I was Deputy Coroner's Aide.
> S. And what were your exact duties?
> G. I was assigned to follow-up on different investigations of deceased persons and also to sign the death certificate.
> S. Under whose supervision did you work?
> G. My immediate supervisor was Richard Rathburn. My overall supervisor was Dr. Theodore Curphey. [Dr. Curphey was the Los Angeles County Coroner at the time.]
> S. Did you work with Dr. Abernathy at any particular time?

G. Dr. Abernathy was in charge of the laboratory department of the L.A. County Coroner's Office which involves toxicology and various laboratory examinations and investigations of coroner's cases.

S. Could you describe to me some of your duties and name the supervisors that you reported to?

G. My duties were, in most cases, to accept 'first calls' on deaths occurring in the County of L.A., that under normal circumstances either did not have a doctor within ten days or died under circumstances that necessitated investigations through the L.A. County Coroner's office and the L.A. City Police Department. My immediate supervisor I reported to was a gentleman by the name of Phil Schwartzburg.

S. Were you the person who signed Marilyn Monroe's final death certificate?

G. Yes, I was.

S. Why did you sign it?

G. I was advised by Dr. Curphey that the death had been determined to be a suicidal death by the "Suicide Squad" who was contacted by the County of Los Angeles.

S. What were your feelings about signing the certificate? You said, I think if I recall, that you were reluctant to sign it?

G. Yes, I was. I felt there was not enough investigation into the case. I also felt there were circumstances of which I had no control of and that Dr. Curphey asked me to sign the death certificate when I wasn't quite sure of exactly what the nature of the death was—or the cause.

S. But you went ahead and signed it upon his direction rather than your own belief or conviction. Is that correct?

G. That is true.

S. After it was signed, were there any significant repercussions or developments as far as the press was concerned?

G. Yes, there was—the press, I would imagine, felt like I did—that a further investigation was necessary. There was a clamor for an inquest into the case. There were also certain insurance that needed clarification and overall there was just a cloud around her death that under normal circumstances a full investigation would have clarified that matter a little more.

[Grandison went on to explain that the Los Angeles County Coroner's office would become involved in any case where the deceased was not at the time under direct care of a medical doctor. He said a medical examiner would check the circumstances of death, and would determine the other factors.]

S. When you found out Marilyn Monroe was dead, what did you do?

G. I immediately ordered her remains into the coroner's office so that a more extensive examination could be made, and as you know, determination as to who was next-of-kin as to property, as to circumstances surrounding the tests could be made, because of the lack of apparent evidence, so that we could come to this conclusion. The only circumstances that could have prevented this natural process from occurring would be circumstances which would determine to be a possible homicide or a possible death at the hands of another. So, under normal circumstances, the Westwood Mortuary would pick up the remains, take the body to their establishment, whereas a deputy medical examiner would be assigned and he would go out to the establishment and make the determination for us.

S. What was it that you saw in particular that

maybe impressed you after Marilyn Monroe's body was brought to the county morgue?

G. The one thing that I remembered at this point in time was that there was a note—that was basically illegible in that we could not determine who had signed it, but there definitely was a note there which might have possibly given the indication that Marilyn Monroe had committed suicide. I could not personally say that it was written by her. Later that note disappeared, within one to two days after that, and it was never in the property [room] again. It began to make me feel as though there might be circumstances that I had no knowledge of that could have made it a shady situation.

S. I talked with you earlier about this note and you mentioned the fact that it might have been a note that Marilyn Monroe had scribbled, the note was not readable—was very scribbly, and in her handwriting allegedly; could this possibly have been a note that she had written, not as a suicide note, but as a final note to maybe notify somebody or tell something to that extent, but was really unrecognizable? Is that correct?

G. That is correct. I could not determine precisely what the note said. But, the fact remains that the note was there, and that obviously whoever wrote it, was writing to communicate to someone, something.

S. Do you remember what the note looked like in the way of correspondence? I mean was the handwriting slanted to the right or up and down or to the left, or what—because Marilyn did write to the extreme right in a looping-type writing which was very illegible even when she was sober.

G. To the best of my recollection the writing was slanted. However, I can't really remember. I couldn't really recall this.

S. Who do you think, in your own opinion, confiscated this particular note which may have been very instrumental as a vital key to her death?

G. The only thing that I can say is that it was someone who had more authority than I or—someone who did not want this note seen past a couple of days it remained in the coroner's property.

S. Do you know what happened to it?

G. No, I don't. The property each night—I mean—each night a different deputy coroner's aide was assigned the case for investigation as to next-of-kin for proper burial and the dissemination of property that we had in our possession. It was put into a safe and the safe was locked each evening as the 8-to-5 shift left. Now it would have had to be someone with a key to the safe. That's all I know.

S. Who had keys to that particular safe?

G. The immediate supervisor which was Chief Deputy Coroner's Aide, Mr. Rathburn and the Coroner of the County L.A., Dr. Theodore Curphey.

S. Was Abernathy and Curphey aware of the note?

G. Yes, they had to be. I don't know if Dr. Curphey was aware of the note. But I would imagine just by the normal course of things that Mr. Rathburn would have informed him of the note and he [Dr. Curphey] would have complete knowledge of what was going on.

[Grandison said the note was put in the file of the Suicide Investigation Team. Grandison was not familiar with Marilyn's handwriting, and could not identify it. He claimed the coroner's office received the note from the Los Angeles Police Department.]

S. When you first saw her body, did you notice

66

anything special, in contrast to maybe other corpses? I mean, that is, discoloration, bruises or were they *really* bruises?

G. It was known at that time by everyone in the coroner's office the fact that she did possess bruises on the back of her thighs. That, in fact, I did see the bruises on the back of her thighs approximately one to three days after her death.

S. Could those possibly have been as other coroner's have said, lividity and not bruises—by lividity, I mean pressures from the lividity, the fact that she possibly could have died on her back and have been flipped over to her anterior side leaving the posture with the discoloration which were interpreted as bruises in contrast to possible lividity?

G. I was informed by Dr. Harold Kade, who was also a medical examiner working in the office at that time, that this could have been very easily the case.

S. What is your interpretation of a body, since your experience in this business, where a body has been on the pressure points like the hips and the back and so forth, and been flipped over to the position that discoloration has set in from the anterior, meaning the front side, and the posterior, meaning the back side, where the discoloration had set in and looked like bruises? Have you ever had experience in that department?

G. Yes, this is determined by the length of time between when a person dies and when the body is discovered. I have ssen many times where after a person has been dead for so long that discoloration automatically takes place, based upon how they are positioned at the time of death.

S. Do you believe that Marilyn's body could have been moved?

G. Based on the evidence that was brought to my attention at the time of her death, it led me to believe that the circumstances surrounding her death were not as they have been reported.

S. Would you mind telling me what you were told?

G. Well, the coroner's offices, at the time I was there, was the place where there was a lot of things happening, a lot of circumstances which I did not understand at the time, but because I was a young person of 21, possibly 22 years old. But I was told that a lot of viewings of the body by employees, police officials, insurance officials, high officials of our department that viewed the body and some could very possibly have had sexual acts with the body.

S. And this was at the old downtown L.A. Coroner's office?

G. It was at the Hall of Justice, at 211 West Temple Street, L.A.

S. And there possibly was intercourse with Marilyn's body by many people at that particular time?

G. Yes, there was.

S. Did unusual activity take place during the time she was in the morgue, in the way of people opening up the, you know, you pull out the drawer that she's in naturally, look at her and so forth, I mean, what were the interests of the people who looked at her including what number one, the insurance men, number two, the studio people you said were there. Did you ever hear of any comments as to what their interests were?

G. Well, obviously, one of the primary interests was the fact that she was a person of notoriety. Because I was one of the individuals in charge of the investigation, the circumstances surrounding her death, also in the circumstances surrounding or determining who was to be acknowledged as to the next-of-kin, I came into a lot of information from individuals as to why they were interested and why they would have the need to view the body and a lot of times I was instructed by Dr. Curphey as to what I should do and I followed those instructions.

S. Now, during that time Dr. Thomas Noguchi performed the autopsy, but did he actually do it himself?

G. I do recall the day of that autopsy and I do know for a fact that Dr. Curphey was there at the autopsy, and therefore, being the Coroner of L.A., I know that he personally supervised everything that happened.

S. Did you see any first reports of the autopsy, meaning the complete reports, and if so, what were they?

G. I do not recall actually the results of the first autopsy report; however, I do recall the first autopsy report that was filed. I was in direct contact with a stenographer who typed up these reports and I do know for a fact that those reports disappeared from the files and were never seen again.

S. Why do you think they disappeared?

G. It could be pure guesswork on my part, but I do know for a fact that what I saw in the first autopsy report was not what I saw in the second which was later listed in terms of presentation to me for signing of the death certificate. They were not, in fact, the same.

S. Who would have the power to possibly change these reports?

G. Dr. Noguchi and Dr. Curphey.

S. Were they influenced by anybody above them, either in Los Angeles or elsewhere, Washington maybe?

G. That could very possibly have been because at the signing of the death certificate, I was called down into Dr. Curphey's office for the signing of this death certificate. I knew at that time that it was really not necessary because my role was something of a matter of just taking the evidence that was presented from me for signing. But at the time of the signing of her death certificate I was called into the office where Dr. Curphey was there—to the best of my recollection a representative of Prudential Insurance Company, a representative from the Los Angeles County District Attorney's office, and some other individuals who I had no knowledge of, which I was told to sign the death certificate so it could be filed and the case would be taken to a different level.

S. Did you sign this on your own volition believing that it was true, or did you do it on orders from the people who told you to sign it?

G. Well, I did not sign it because I thought that the circumstances were true. I signed it because I was told that the evidence surrounding the case had been determined to be true at the time of my signing.

S. If we could regress a minute, as I understand it, first the death certificate was made out not signed but the cause of death was made out number one a "suicide," second, about a week or so later it was made out as "possible suicide," and third, the one you signed was "probable suicide." Probable suicide, according to what the coroner's office told me, is that it means the person who died, really meaning Marilyn Monroe, committed suicide accidentally. Now there are three changes. Could you enlighten me as to why it was changed three times?

G. The first two death certificates that were issued were what was called "pending" death certificates. That meant that there were investigations being carried out at the time of those findings that might lead to a determination at a later date that may not be in keeping with that which was signed at that particular time. Under normal circumstances, those death certificates would have been signed merely for the burial of the individual who was deceased. So the terminology that was there, could have either been political or just expedient in terms of signing the death certificate.

S. Did you have apprehensions about signing the last certificate of her death?

G. I had been receiving at the signing her death certificate an average of thirty-five to forty calls a day that I was talking to, and there is no telling how many inquiries that had been coming into the office that had never reached me, in terms of informing the coroner's office that further determination or investigation should be made in order to come up with the truth of this matter. Because of that situation, and because of the circumstances surrounding it, and because of the fact that I was not sure what had happened, no, I was not completely sure that the death certificate was in fact a true certificate of an investigation.

S. The final verdict on her [Marilyn Monroe's] death certificate you signed was "probable suicide." Do you feel that that was fair? Or do you feel that is what it really was?

G. Well, based upon the fact that another area that we have not gone into, was the fact that there were two or three different police reports that were filed with the Coroner of Los Angeles at that time, there is no way in the world that myself as an individual and signer of that certificate, could have made that determination because the facts were not all in. Another individual that was at that meeting at Dr. Curphey's office was a representative of the Suicide Team that investigated all suicides in the County of Los Angeles. He was unsure, but he sided with Dr. Curphey, and his presentation to me, which they had determined this death to be a suicide.

S. Now, Marilyn Monroe was a very famous movie actress as we all know, and when a star of her status was found dead under mysterious circumstances—the question I'd like to ask you is *why was there no inquest?*

G. ...It would not have been normal to have an inquest in a case such as Marilyn Monroe. However, the circumstances in my opinion, warranted some other investigation besides the natural or the normal flow which would have been the Suicide Squad in the determination made by the laboratory under Dr. Abernathy and the medical examiner which would have been Dr. Thomas Noguchi.

S. Was there ever pressure upon the coroner's office from the immediate press and television and radio and so forth, or the general news media, for an inquest?

G. Initially, that was the case, but then, you know the press normally looks for the sensationalism of a situation. Therefor they normally clamor under that type of situation for an inquest. However, as the item became stagnant and no longer was a determining factor as to what the situation was, the news media eventually stopped trying to figure out what caused her death. They expected Dr. Curphey to have a press conference immediately after that, within a couple of days after the body had reached the coroner's office. He said that there was no doubt, and that was far before any investigation could have been out, he stated that at that time there was no doubt that Miss Monroe had committed suicide.

S. What did he base it upon? Do you remember?

G. He based it upon the fact that certain

individuals were interviewed, and there is no telling who they might have been—they could have very easily been the Suicide Team, but individuals could have been the L.A.P.D. But these individuals had stated that Marilyn had been despondent and had indicated at times that she was going to take her own life.

S. Was there any real evidence to the fact that she tried to take her own life before?

G. No, there was none.

S. What people, either insurance or possibly maybe from the studio, actually came down to the coroner's office during the time her body was there, and who did they talk to and why did they come down?

G. I personally can recall the Prudential Insurance Company talking to me on numerous occasions about when we were going to finalize the death certificate and how the determination was going to be made, as to what her cause of death was, and to the best of my recollection, as I say, talk was going around pretty strong at that time. I can remember people telling me about other people asking and wanting to know. And you know, the general office talk surrounding a case like that. But, I myself personally, the only contact I had was with the Prudential Insurance Company and a couple of times with insurance personnel wanting to know what exactly was happening. I mean *not* insurance personnel but rather the studio personnel.

S. To your knowledge, was she insured by Prudential at that time?

G. Based upon the fact that the Prudential Insurance Company was there in Dr. Curphey's office, at the time when he instructed me to sign the death certificate, it indicated to me that obviously there were some insurance claims being made in regard to her death.

S. You were asked to sign Marilyn Monroe's death certificate. You were *the* person who signed it, correct?

G. That's correct.

S. Was there any protest on your part, meaning you were following orders, or was there something that came across the desk and you signed it as a matter of record, so to speak?

G. I was instructed to sign it. My comment at that time was the fact that I did not know *why* the circumstances existed that would bring me into the office for that type of situation for me to sign the death certificate. It could have been, in fact, been sent down the normal road, that situations such as this would take, and an individual would have signed it without even giving it a second thought. However, the fact that they called me down in that office, and instructed me to sign it, led me to believe that this was something outside of the normal course of the coroner's business.

S. Now, tell me about the personal items you told me that were brought in from her [Marilyn Monroe's] home and placed on the desk of your boss, who was Dr. Theodore Curphey, the coroner and what were they in your opinion as you saw them, and what possibly happened to them?

G. As much the same as the mysterious note, came in—okay, let me relive that day—the property came into the office under normal circumstances.

[Grandison claimed there was a "discrepancy" from the initial police report regarding the personal items of Marilyn Monroe. The items that were brought into his office was not listed on the police report. He said her property began to disappear "little by little" over the course of a few days. When they released her property, only a few articles were found.]

S. Do you remember any particular articles in the personal possessions that were brought in or what they might have consisted of?

G. I do remember that there was a book that looked like a red diary. There were also a couple of pieces of jewelry. I don't recall if they were deemed to be valuable, because normally valuable property was treated a little differently, than either middle property, or you know, no value property. I don't recall that, but I do recall that there was a diary there and I do recall there were a few pieces of jewelry that to the best of my recollection were not there when the next-of-kin, was finally determined and the property was turned over to them.

S. Who decided not to have an inquest?

G. That would have been Mr. Charles Langhauser, who was the inquest deputy at that time.

S. Why was a Suicide Team called in to investigate the case rather than an inquest? Did you ever see the report that they made?

G. I never saw the report that they had.

S. Now, regarding the police reports—did you ever see the original reports in contrast to the two reports, the original police report and the follow-up police report?

G. Okay, I saw the supplemental police report, to the best of my recollection this was *not* the same police report that I originally saw, because the initial police report that was filed with the L.A.P.D. gave specific indication that there was a suicide note and, the other two police reports, including the police report that was in the file at the time that I signed the death certificate, gave no indication of this note.

S. Do you believe that there possibly was a police cover-up in this whole thing on Marilyn Monroe?

      G. There's no doubt in my mind that the evidence
at the scene of the death were not the same that
were reported to the L.A. County Coroner.

Grandison went on to explain, throughout part of the transcript, that there were certain unusual procedures that were done with regard to the Marilyn Monroe case, that normally had not taken place with other deceased individuals. He definitely stated that he thought the insurance played a major part in the determination of her cause of death at the L.A. County Coroner's Office, for it was no secret that insurance companies and morticians, during the holiday season, brought cases of liquor into the coroner's office and also presented generous gifts to the coroner's officials that, in his opinion, could sway their determinations, at times of various deaths, as to the removal of bodies, as to the eventual signing of death certificates, and as to determination of causes of death.

He also stated that the entire coroner's office, at the level of deputies, which included medical examiners, deputy coroner's aides, and supervisory personnel, received generous gifts from morticians, insurance companies and other individuals. Asked about Dr. Thomas Noguchi, who had been accused of not testing the lower intestine, because he did not have the facilities for doing so, Grandison stated that although he was not a medical man, he did realize that the County of Los Angeles had all the facilities needed to take any type of a test that had to be made, providing they wanted to make it. However, he emphasized the fact the Dr. Noguchi did not have the final determination of what was to be done and what was not to be done. He said he knew for a fact that Dr. Theodore Curphey handled and made all determinations that applied to the Marilyn Monroe case. He also stated that Dr. Curphey took personal charge of Marilyn's case, and any questions regarding her demise had to come from him directly.

Grandison also stated that they had tried to contact the next-of-kin, naming Arthur Miller as the first one to contact because of his position, and because of his credibility to take charge of her body for burial purposes, but not for the dissemination of her property. However, according to Grandison, Miller failed to respond to any of their inquiries. He stated that the next person they decided to contact was Joe DiMaggio, who at first refused to have anything to do with claiming Marilyn's body. (It might be a note of interest here that a body, without a next-of-kin available, has to be "claimed" by either a friend or the next-of-kin in order to remove it from the coroner's office to the funeral home.) Grandison admitted making most of these phone calls himself, hoping to get somebody to claim the body to give Marilyn a decent burial.

The following statements from Grandison proved to be of further interest:

> S. Would you say that you might have been substantially pressured to sign that certificate [Marilyn Monroe's death certificate] against your will?
>
> G. There's no doubt about it. Had I a choice, I would not want to be involved in it, because of the fact of the phone calls, because of the fact that I had personally seen the note, because of the fact that the investigation by the police department was inconclusive and I could not get the necessary information that was necessary for me to come to a conclusion—not that my conclusion would have been overridden the conclusion of the medical examiner who ultimately would have had to make the final determination. However, the medical examiner had not signed the death certificate. The signing of the death certificate was left in the hands of

the administrative offices of the county coroner's office, which ultimately fell into my hands. I would not have signed the death certificate without the information that I had requested from the police department.

S. Do you believe in your opinion, after all these years have passed, that Marilyn Monroe really, by her own hand, committed suicide?

G. *I do not believe that she committed suicide.* And that's due to the fact that the normal process again, that come through the coroner's office, and the teamwork at the L.A.P.D. or the L.A. Sheriff's Department and the Los Angeles Coroner's Office and all medical personnel which in most cases are doctors, normally send in and normally get the information at some point in time to where you can make proper conclusions. That process did not occur in Miss Monroe's case. The police department was reluctant. They submitted a police report, withdrew the police report, submitted another police report in lieu of the note, in lieu of the pill bottles, in lieu of the fact that Dr. Engelberg, was that his words were thought to be a symbol of the truth that were not investigated, I do not believe.

S. In your opinion, would you say that Marilyn Monroe died of suicide or would you say that she might have been murdered?

G. Indications were by some of the people who were closely involved in the investigation in Miss Monroe's case, indications from them would lead me to believe that the death was other than a suicide.

S. Was there ever any mention of murder mentioned in the coroner's office?

G. Yes.

S. Do you remember by whom?

G. No, I don't.

S. But that did come up?

G. Numerous times.

S. Was it among a certain group of people that was, say, in a clandestine, in the sense not to talk to anybody else, or was it sort of among a large group of people?

G. Well, at that time the name of Mr. Robert Kennedy was mentioned. Of course, based upon that time and date, no one would want to go any further than mention it. It became a joke of the office. However, they were people not within the coroner's office, but people who came to the office looking for information that we were gathering, that indicated to myself and to other people in the coroner's office, that there was definitely an effort on the behalf of some people to kill Miss Monroe for one reason or another.

S. Do you know what that reason may have been or did you hear what the reason might have been?

G. The indications were that it was something that she had known or heard or something like that—or been involved in.

After this interview with Lionel Grandison, we did check throught the county files and discovered that at the time of Marilyn Monroe's death, he was actually employed as a deputy coroner's aide. Furthermore, matching his current signature with the signature on Marilyn Monroe's death certificate showed that he was the one and the same person, as the signatures were identical. We had every reason to believe that Lionel Grandison was telling the truth.

Although this chapter contains only the significant portions of the interview, certain other portions were deleted only because they were somewhat repetitious and dealt with various medical situations, such as the inventory of the pill bottles that came in, how the autopsy was done, and various aspects of which Grandison, not being a doctor, admitted that he could not know about. Basically, the information that Grandison supplied us threw quite an interesting new light upon the workings of the coroner's office. We concluded that Dr. Thomas Noguchi had done a reasonable job as a forensic pathologist, but we must remember that it was Dr. Theodore Curphey, the coroner at the time, who not only supervised Marilyn's autopsy, but also took command of the whole situation. According to Grandison, and other people we have talked with associated with various coroner's offices, including Los Angeles, this was highly uncommon.

In analying Grandison's testimony, the following points should be made:

1. It was Lionel Grandison who "foiled the suicide plot," and who ordered Marilyn Monroe's body from Westwood Memorial Cemetery to the downtown coroner's office. (Had this not been done, there would have been no autopsy, and obviously no conflicting statements as to the cause of her death today.)

2. Grandison confirmed the fact that there was an alleged suicide note, or some scribbled message, allegedly attributed to Marilyn's handwriting, which disappeared from the locker in which her personal possessions were kept. (This indicates another fault in the coroner's office, meaning the indiscreet manner in which procedures were done.)

3. As we had discovered in our past investigation, Grandison confirmed the fact that there were several bruises over Marilyn's body, which were not listed on the autopsy report that was available to the public.

4. Grandison confirmed the fact that there were three verdicts of suicide; that is, one of "suicide?" [Which was a notation that Sergeant Jack Clemmons made in his report handed over to Sergeant Robert Byron, who concluded the case), a second one of "possible suicide?", and then the

third and final one, which is on record as the cause of death, which is "probable suicide."

5. Grandison also revealed the fact that he was "forced" to sign Marilyn Monroe's death certificate *against* his will. (Please note that the death certificate does not contain the usual dossier of information, which any individual in a coroner's office signing a death certificate is required to read under state law, to determine if the cause of death listed on the certificate is proper. Grandison was never given this opportunity.)

6. Grandison confirmed the fact that there was talk of "murder" in those first twenty-four hours after he had ordered Marilyn Monroe's body downtown to the coroner's office.

7. Grandison confirmed that he had seen, opened, and read parts of Marilyn's "red diary," in an attempt to locate her next-of-kin, only to discover the names of both President John F. Kennedy and Attorney General Robert Kennedy listed in this book, plus the name of Fidel Castro, and other information pertaining to the United States government.

8. Grandison confirmed the fact that the name of Bobby Kennedy was mentioned numerous times within the first twenty-four hours while Marilyn's body was in the coroner's office.

9. Grandison established the fact that the majority of Marilyn's personal possessions, brought into the coroner's office, disappeared before her body was even released to Westwood Memorial Park Cemetery for burial. (It must be remembered here, that this unethical procedure, i.e., rampant misconduct in the coroner's office, is one of the major charges made by the Los Angeles County Board of Supervisors against Dr. Thomas Noguchi in early 1982, which removed him from his position as Los Angeles County Coroner, and which he is appealing.)

10. In the information Grandison furnished, he alluded to the fact that other persons than those in the coroner's office, such as studio people, insurance representatives, and other powerful individuals, took a great interest in the fact the Dr. Theodore Curphey deemed Marilyn Monroe to be a "suicide."

11. Grandison admitted having first-hand knowledge of certain members of the staff at the coroner's office who were necrophiliacs, who violated Marilyn's body before the autopsy was made.

12. Grandison verified the fact that there were many, many people, from all walks of life, who were admitted openly into the storage vaults, where Marilyn Monroe's body was kept in Crypt Number 33, and who viewed the body for either curiosity or other purposed. (It might be pointed out here that this fact has recently been verified by a well-known photographer, Leigh Weiner, who allowed the Los Angeles *Times*, in its Sunday Calendar section in September 1982, to run one of the several dozen photographs of Marilyn Monroe in the drawer of Crypt Number 33.)

VII

The Man Who Would Take Hoover's Job

Adding to the mysterious circumstances in which Marilyn Monroe was found dead, there followed a few more strange events while her embalmed body lay in a cold-storage vault, waiting to be claimed. As noted before, a deceased body, under such circumstances, has to be "claimed" before it can be transported to the funeral home for preparation and burial. On Monday morning, August 6, nobody had claimed Marilyn's body. But there was some quiet activity going on not too distant from her sealed house in Brentwood.

The Brentwood office of General Telephone Company had barely opened when two well-dressed men entered, flashed some very proper credentials with badges, and requested Marilyn Monroe's telephone records. Less than five minutes later, Marilyn's complete log was handed to the two men, who took possession of them and left the office.

My client, Bob Slatzer, had heard about this a couple weeks later through his good friends Florabel Muir and

Walter Winchell, both top columnists at the time, and both interested in the Monroe case. Muir was the first to tell Slatzer that Marilyn's telephone records had been confiscated and were in the possession of Chief William H. Parker of the Los Angeles Police Department. Parker had even boasted to Muir that he had Marilyn's telltale telephone records, which listed all of her calls for the past summer—and most importantly, that last month of her life.

Chief Parker had actually "flashed" the records in front of Florabel Muir, and from what her eyes could gather, it left no doubt in her mind that they were original telephone records, for she saw Marilyn Monroe's name and phone number on the first page. Parker, who ran the police department with an iron hand, in the opinion of many, including Sergeant Jack Clemmons, boasted to Florabel that those phone records are "my ticket to get Hoover's job when Bobby Kennedy becomes President."

Slatzer had confirmed this with Winchell, who speculated that perhaps Parker's boys had confiscated the records for Bobby Kennedy, but instead of giving them to him Parker had decided to hold onto them and turn them over to Bobby when he got the seat in the oval office. One thing is certain: the telephone records would show Bobby's private number less than ten days before Marilyn's death, plus all the other calls to Hyannisport and even to the White House. Add to that the local calls to her doctors, studio, and Pat Newcomb—plus perhaps other calls that were never to be made public.

It was not difficult to speculate what anyone would want with Marilyn's telephone records. Perhaps the most incriminating of all the calls these records covered were the ones made from her house between the time that she actually died and the time that the police were notified. Those could be very interesting, for it seemed like a lot of calling was going on before anyone actually thought about informing the police.

Going right to the source, my client questioned a spokesman at General Telephone, whose offices in 1962 were in Brentwood before the company moved into a spacious new office building in Santa Monica, where they are located today.

The spokesman for General Telephone Company told Slatzer that there was some speculation that Marilyn's records had "disappeared out of their office."

Being more specific, my client asked, "How did they disappear?"

"Somebody just came in and took them," the man replied.

"Who would this 'somebody' be?" Slatzer questioned.

"Look," the man replied, somewhat exasperated, "All I know is what I have been told. Two 'well-dressed' men came in here right after we opened that day and asked to see her records."

"Who were they?"

"I don't know. They showed official badges and identification and they were given the records."

"To look at or to take with them?" Slatzer asked.

"I assume to look at," the man replied. "They took a quick look at them and then went out the door, taking the records with them."

"Didn't anybody try to stop them?" Slatzer asked.

"I guess not," the man answered.

"Isn't that against the law?"

"I believe it is," the man replied. "Look, we've been getting nothing but a lot of phone calls about this, and I've told you all I know."

"What was the name of the employee who turned over these records?" Slatzer asked.

"Nobody seems to know," the man answered in a resigned voice. "Why?"

"If I could find out *who* gave the records to these men,"

Slatzer explained, "perhaps I could get an identification."

"I can't tell you anything else. I've taken too much time on this already," the man sighed.

My client pressed the man a little bit more, asking him if he could possibly question some of the clerks on duty that morning of a little over two weeks before, but was told that could not be arranged.

"Could it have been an inside job?" Slatzer asked.

That was it! My client was asked to leave. The most interesting thing about this confrontation was that the spokesman for the telephone company did not ask for identification—he must have assumed that Slatzer was just another reporter.

Before going out to the General Telephone Company, Slatzer checked out the law on obtaining a person's telephone records. In 1934, the Federal Communications Act was passed, which prohibited the release of information on any subscriber to a third party. The only exception is that the FBI can obtain the records if a lawful demand is verified and an order signed by a judge. In the State of California, there is also Penal Code Section 830, which allows any local authorities to *view* an individual's telephone records. All that is required under that law is a written order from the chief of police or sheriff of a county, and a court order signed by a presiding judge. Even then, an individual's telephone records are only available if the subscriber is involved in an existing criminal case or suspected of a criminal action, which Marilyn Monroe was not.

After my client had come to me, and I had taken on this case, I personally retraced a lot of his footsteps. I made a contact at General Telephone Company.

My source told me that he was personally at the telephone company on August 6, 1962, but the news of the records being confiscated didn't surface right away. It took about a week before reporters started calling. By that

86

time, according to my source, nobody admitted giving out her records, for that would have been highly illegal. He also admitted that the company had taken a lot of criticism over the event, and stringent memos had been issued immediately about releasing any information on telephone records without clearing it with a supervisor of the company.

"We do know that Miss Monroe's records were taken from the old Brentwood office," he told me, "but by the time our special agents investigated, nobody owned up to handing them over. We have a lot of people working here, so the damage was done. We just made sure it would never happen again."

Winchell had told Slatzer that it had been a good investigative effort on his part to make a personal call on the telephone company, but thought it did sound like an inside job, or that whoever handed the records over was afraid to admit it. The fact that there was already a cover-up about Marilyn's death, Winchell reasoned, was all the more reason that the killers would go a bit further and confiscate the rest of the evidence—the telephone records.

There were other reporters who were very much aware of the missing telephone records, but their investigation into General Telephone proved fruitless. Dorothy Kilgallen was one who couldn't get any information. Another was James Hudson, former news editor of United Press International, who had gained newspaper fame by covering the Hiss, Frank Costello and Rosenberg trials, as well as the Andrea Doria and many major airline crashes. This news veteran of twenty years (as of 1967) also hit a dead end with the telephone records.

One thing I can say is that Slatzer had guts, for he personally visited Chief Parker's office, unannounced, about noon one day, and accidentally caught the chief coming out of his office. His main purpose was to make an appointment with Parker to discuss the missing telephone records.

Noon, as Slatzer knew from his newspaper days, was always a good time to find out things. Secretaries breeze out to lunch, and their replacements are often late. Slatzer saw Chief Parker and asked him directly if he could make an appointment to see him. Parker asked what he wanted, and Slatzer said he would like to talk with him about Marilyn's missing telephone records. According to Slatzer, Parker did a double-take and replied that he didn't have any information on that subject. When Slatzer brazenly told Parker he had heard Marilyn's records were in his office, Parker asked, "Just who in the hell are you?"

"Just a friend. My name's Bob Slatzer," he answered.

"A friend of who?" Parker asked.

"Marilyn Monroe."

"Well, somebody's given you a bum steer. I don't know what you're talking about." And Parker stormed out of his office.

The most interesting observation here is that, in their first confrontation, Parker did not deny he had Marilyn's records. It was only at the end of their conversation that Parker brushed the whole matter aside.

Analyzing why Chief Parker kept these records in his office, and was even boasting about them to some news reporters, we find he had a very good reason. The two Kennedy brothers had planned to oust J. Edgar Hoover from his job as head of the FBI, and at one point came very close.

After Marilyn's death, and sometime before JFK was assasinated (November 1963), President Kennedy invited the Director of the FBI and Bobby Kennedy to a special luncheon in the White House. The bothers Kennedy had laid out some very good plans. A letter of resignation was in an envelope JFK carried to the luncheon and placed on the table beside him. They were going to get Hoover's resignation that day, because they had certain things they were going to tell Hoover which, if brought out to the public, would force his resignation. However, Hoover came well-prepared, for he had a large Manila envelope too, which he placed at his side during the luncheon.

When the time came for JFK to get down to business and break a few things to Hoover, the old director reached into his large envelope and gave one dossier to the President and another to Bobby. Then he continued to eat his lunch. As both of the Kennedys read the detailed pages, which reportedly contained reports of their extra-curricular love affairs and government dealings, JFK could not finish his lunch and Bobby was about ready to throw up. President Kennedy got up from the table first, taking his large Manila envelope with him, never giving it to Hoover, and Bobby followed.

"I assume you have copies of these files," JFK said, forcing a smile.

Hoover nodded, now starting his dessert, suddenly finding himself alone at the table. It might be of great interest at this time to state that there was some information on Marilyn's death, and her dating both Kennedys in the file. Hoover revered Marilyn Monroe and kept a large painting of her in his home, prominently displayed along the staircase wall.

Not only did Hoover have the goods on the brothers Kennedy—what they were doing, the women they were seeing—but Hoover's work started back when JFK was a senator and Bobby was still following big brother's footsteps. By the time of the 1960 election, Hoover had gathered so much evidence on the Kennedys that he could have caused JFK to lose the election without a doubt. In his files were the affairs of JFK with Marilyn Monroe, among a host of others. Bobby's amours, as brief as they were at the time, were also listed. It just might be of interest to the students of history that Hoover had been keeping files on JFK from the time he got out of the Navy and began swinging around in Hollywood in the late forties, living with actor Robert Stack for awhile.

In 1960, J. Edgar Hoover reportedly offered these files to Richard Nixon to use as a weapon against John F. Kennedy. Nixon, a gentleman in the opinion of those who deeply knew him, glanced at the files and told Hoover he felt that would be "dirty politics." History could have been different had Nixon decided to use those files.

As we all know, Nixon lost the 1960 election to John Kennedy, one of the first things JFK did when taking residence in the White House was vow to get Hoover—for he found out what Hoover had tried to do to him in 1960. That's how this confrontation had started, much to President Kennedy's dismay.

If Chief Parker ever thought he could take Hoover's place as director of the FBI, it certainly would not have been under JFK's administration, nor even Bobby's had he lived long enough to attain the presidency. Hoover had too much on both of the Kennedy boys, and they knew it. Chief Parker was not a naive man, yet the brother of the President of the United States allegedly made Parker such a promise, which isn't to be taken lightly. Parker actually believed Bobby. Obviously, Bobby even believed himself that he could unseat Hoover. But if big brother Jack had failed, what chance would Bobby have? However, Parker was taking no chances in holding his ace—the possession of the Monroe telephone records.

Just what would those records tell, other than what we have already covered?

First of all, direct distance dialing had not been installed in Los Angeles in 1962, and every long distance call made was listed. From where Marilyn lived at that time, every toll call would have been listed. So even if she did not place those last several calls herself and it is obvious that she did not—they would have shown up on her record.

After Slatzer's initial visit to Parker, he again attempted to reach him by telephone and succeeded. This time, Parker's answer was quite different. Slatzer, identifying himself as a leg man for Florabel Muir, asked if he could see Marilyn's telephone bills.

This time Parker did not deny having them; instead, he told Slatzer, "Florabel's already seen them. Why has she got you calling me?" Then he hung up the phone.

On July 16, 1966, Chief Parker was receiving a standing ovation from more than a thousand Marine Corps veterans in the Pacific Ballroom of the Statler-Hilton Hotel, when he leaned back in his chair and started gasping. He was rushed to Central Receiving Hospital, and died about forty minutes later at the age of 64.

Before Chief Parker's funeral, it was reported that Marilyn's telephone records had been confiscated from his office, and that is the last that anyone ever heard of them.

However, in my file on Marilyn's missing telephone records, this is the key information that verifies three things:

(a) Her records were confiscated from the offices of General Telephone in the early morning hours of August 6, 1962.

(b) Chief William Parker was the custodian of those records for nearly fourteen years.

(c) There was an apparent cover-up in the Los Angeles Police Department—namely, Chief William Parker.

Like the red diary, if Marilyn's telephone records could be located even after all of these years—if they still exist—they too could tell us a lot more about her killers.

Being an optimist, though still dealing in reality rather than rumors, I feel that perhaps either of these records—or information leading to them—just might surface one of these days.

Interestingly enough, maybe somebody else even has copies. Maybe Marilyn's phone records are part of the secret F.B.I. file!

VIII
Marilyn Monroe's F.B.I. Files

When the Freedom of Information Act was in effect, and after we had discovered that certain F.B.I. files were kept on Marilyn Monroe, both before and after her death, we made an attempt to obtain copies of those files. The big question here is why Marilyn Monroe, an actress by profession, had been the subject of investigation by the Federal Bureau of Investigation. She had never been involved in any criminal activity, her only confrontation with the police being some unpaid parking tickets, so we decided to track down and find out what these reports contained. Of course, we supposed, as we were later to find, that one report focused upon her marriage and relationship with playwright Arthur Miller, who in 1956 was subpoenaed before a government committee investigating his possible Communist ties.

If you have never tried to locate information through the Freedom of Information Act, I would advise against it unless you have a lot of time, patience and persistence. If your application, as designed by the United States Department of Justice, does not have an "i" dotted, or a spaced checked, or a signature in the correct place, or contain the reason you really want the information on an individual, they can send it back for any one of these reasons and more as late as two months later.

If you are successful in filling in all the correct information in the petition, you will receive a formal letter of acknowledgment from the Office of the Associate Attorney General, assigning you a case number and advising you that their office has a substantial background of appeals and that you will have to await your turn.

Since our request had to be made through an individual who could legitimately state the reason he wanted Marilyn's files, we decided to file everything under Robert F. Slatzer's name and address. His reason was that the information seeked out would be for literary research, which it was. This was under oath, and we were not lying.

Together, Slatzer and I became the architects of a pattern of requests, one right after another, and many only through filing an appeal after the original request had been denied. This meant filling out more forms, stating why we felt we were entitled to information previously denied, and then receiving back a confirmation that the appeal was under advisement.

A letter from the office of David G. Flanders, Chief of Information-Privacy Acts Branch, Records Management Division, United States Department of Justice, Federal Bureau of Investigation, consisted of three pages, the first two of which had boxes checked for processing. One such box noted that Slatzer had to furnish the date and birth of the subject of his inquiry, meaning Marilyn Monroe. (Picture the FBI, holding records on Marilyn Monroe and not knowing her date and year of birth or where she was born!)

Another box was checked that required a notarized signature, although that was not mentioned on this particular request form. But the most interesting paragraph which shed more light to out investigation, read:

"Please be advised that references pertaining to the late Marilyn Monroe are voluminous. We are not quite sure as to the scope of your request. Are you requesting any and all information which we have pertaining to her, or do you wish only that information pertaining to where your name may be connected with her? Please clarify your request."

At the end of about two months, a few pages from one file arrived. They had been heavily edited, meaning that over 50% of the investigative material could not be read, for it was "leaded out," as they say in investigative circles. There were notations such as: "3 pages have been withheld in their entirety" and "Pages deleted under exemption 67C with no segregable material for release." These indicated the portions not even provided and the balance received was highly edited. However, references to Norman Mailer's book were mentioned; so were the names of other authors, with the F.B.I.'s stated feelings, most of which were negative, about their findings. One item dealt with the missing telephone records. The F.B.I. said flatly: "This is false and neither the files of the Los Angeles Office nor F.B.I. Headquarters indicate the existence of any such tapes."

Further references, highly edited, refer to the Kennedys, who were reportedly at odds with the F.B.I. and the C.I.A. because after the Bay of Pigs, President Kennedy was moving to limit the power of these agencies. Then are a lot of "blacked-out" paragraphs.

Many pages are from the desk of J. Edgar Hoover, but the names of agents who were to receive the memos are mostly "blacked-out."

Information in this first file—and I say "first" only

because we were to discover through additional appeals that there were several more files on Marilyn Monroe—is from memos coming into Washington, D.C., from F.B.I. agents all over the country.

One section goes into the background of Walter Winchell, including clips of articles he wrote about Marilyn's death, with check marks against the names of several agents to whom copies had been sent.

Another page mentions Joe DiMaggio's name and concludes:

"...Joe DiMaggio is the only one who remains faithful that the man who killed Miss Monroe is still at large and can never be arrested. But wherever he goes, whatever he touches, whomever he sees; he thinks of Marilyn. His guilt never leaves him, his fear has become his friend."

Then there is a special notation at the bottom of this page that reads:

RECOMMENDATION:
For Information

This is followed by some illegible initials.

Through a nearly two year period, through a series of appeals and correspondence that dragged out to what seemed to be an eternity, eight separate files were obtained.

Finally, in a letter dated June 20, 1980, regarding our last available chance to appeal for additional information, we received a letter from John H. Shenefield, Associate Attorney General, at the United States Department of Justice, denying access to any further material through that department.

The letter read in part:

"...After careful consideration of your appeal, I have decided to affirm the initial action on this case. Certain of the material pertaining to Ms. Monroe is classified and I am affirming the denial of access to it on the basis of 5 U.S.C. 552 (b) (1). The Department Review Committee has determined that this material warrants continued classification under Executive Order 12065. Other materials were properly withheld from you pursuant to 5 U.S.C. 552 (b) (6), (7) (c) and (7) D. These provisions pertain to materials the release of which would constitute a clearly unwarranted invasion of the personal privacy of a third party and to investigatory records compiled for law enforcement purposes, the release of which would, respectively, constitute an unwarranted invasion of privacy of third parties and disclose the identities of confidential sources. None of the information being withheld is appropriate for discretionary release."

But there's more—the last paragraph is quite interesting:

"...Judicial review of my action on this appeal is available to you in the United States District Court for the judicial district in which you reside or have your principal place of business, or in the District of Columbia, which is also where the records you seek are located."

In other words, finding out what our government is really not telling from their files on Marilyn Monroe would take an appeal to the United States Supreme Court. Just what are they hiding even at this late date?

In tallying the pages received, we find over half of each one, if not more, is "blacked-out" as "classified," And in each file there are "inserts" that list anywhere from two to nine pages deleted in their entirety. Why?

We hope to find out. Ironically, when the Los Angeles County District Attorney's office is investigating the cause of her death, we have the Department of Justice suppressing a tremendous amount of information about Marilyn Monroe.

If the case is to be viewed fairly, this information should be released—even if a Congressional action has to take place.

We have come this far in getting Marilyn's death investigated, and the authorities now realize it was a little more than a suicide. Without material from the Department of Justice, no investigation can ever be complete. I do not believe it is fair to withhold this information when it could determine how Marilyn Monroe was killed.

I now question just how much of the F.B.I.'s undisclosed files relate to Marilyn's famous red diary.

IX

$150,000 for Red Diary

Marilyn paid about two dollars for a blank red diary in the summer of 1962. Twenty years later, I was to announce that Nick Harris Detectives would offer $10,000 for the not-so-blank diary. Within forty-eight hours of the offer, a Beverly Hills fine-arts dealer skyrocketed the diary's value up to $100,000. As of August 19,1982, the latest offer stood at $150,000.

John Bowen and Chris Harris, representing the Beverly Hills firm, reported that if they obtained the diary, their mysterious client would share his "find" with me. I had my doubt as to just why someone would pay such an enormous price.

I first learned of the diary in 1972, when my client, Bob, told me Marilyn had showed it to him not long before her death. The last person to read part of it was the deputy coroner's aide, Lionel Grandison, who signed her death certificate under "duress" and verified the diary's contents as described earlier by Slatzer.

If Marilyn had "told all," as she threatened to do at the news conference scheduled for the Monday following her demise, all hell would have broken loose. The top secret information to which she was apparently privy could have caused an international scandal greater that the Teapot Dome, and would have been more devastating than Watergate.

The history of the World may have been changed. It could have sparked World War III, or at the very least created an explosive situation with Cuba and Russia. During a recent news conference, my client stated, "She was carrying around a time-bomb." It could have been John Kennedy, not Richard Nixon, to become the first U.S. President to resign from the office. The aspirations of Robert Kennedy to succeed his brother would have been shattered. And as for Marilyn, those cryptic notes in her red diary, coupled together with the deadly knowledge she possessed, could very well have led to her murder.

The international attention and pandemonium regarding her diary was perhaps brought about by an article I co-authored with Shelley Ross, former producer of the "Today Show." The story appeared in *US Magazine*, entitled, "Who Killed Marilyn Monroe?" and hit the newsstands just prior to the twentieth anniversary of her death. The article capsulized my ten-year investigation with some mention of the red diary.

Slatzer and I were inundated with requests for more information by the world-wide press. I decided to hold a news conference at the Los Angeles Press Club on August 4, 1982, the day before the anniversary of Marilyn's death. I had hoped that the more extensive information I would relate at the conference would end the demands made by the media. But the conference only increased the hundreds of requests for interviews and television appearances.

During the news conference, I demanded that an official

investigation be made, and called for a coroner's inquest.
No inquest had ever been conducted. This was my key
point, but the media chose to emphasize the missing
diary, making it the major issue. The news moved on all
the wire services worldwide, and my conference was
covered by all network television and radio news
programs.

The diary wasn't new evidence. My client detailed it in
1974, in his hardcover book, *The Life and Curious Death
of Marilyn Monroe.* This best-seller was published by
Pinnacle Books, and returned to the presses many times,
selling nearly a million copies in hard and soft cover. Why
now has the media become so interested in the diary?

In late 1979, we had further substantiated the contents
of the diary by interviewing Lionel Grandison, who, in
August 1982, admitted to the news media that our reports
were accurate and that the diary was "stolen" forty-eight
hours after it arrived at the coroner's office. More bizarre
than its disappearance, he said, was the fact that it had
been struck from the official property list. The coroner's
aide had sent someone from his office to Marilyn's house
to search for information that might lead to the nearest
kin. When he first saw the diary, he thought it was an
address book. It turned out to be a stick of dynamite, and
he did not want to become involved. Therefore, his
knowledge was kept secret for eighteen years.

We surmised that many forgeries of the diary would
surface, so intentionally we limited the "known"
contents, verified by both Slatzer and Grandison, to the
following:

> The diary made references to Jack and
> Bobby Kennedy's intimate relationship with
> Marilyn; her knowledge of the Bay of Pigs in
> detail and of the C.I.A. plan to assassinate the
> President of Cuba, Fidel Castro, through the
> use of gangsters.

I said that the Castro assassination attempt did not become public knowledge until 1975, when reported by Senator Frank Church, at a senate investigation devised to discover the covert actions of the C.I.A.

Marilyn's diary contained even more spectacular information—such as Bobby Kennedy's planning to put that "S.O.B." Jimmy Hoffa behind bars; Bobby's vow to cause actor Frank Sinatra to lose his Nevada gambling license at Cal-Neva Lodge because of his alleged associations with underworld figures; Bobby's telling Marilyn how our government, mentioning the C.I.A., was not going to give sanctuary to President Diem of South Viet Nam; names such as Sam Giancanna (Mafia head of Chicago) and Johnny Roseli (another mobster out of Florida who frequented Las Vegas) being on the payroll of the Justice Department, along with other minor underworld names. There was even a notation Marilyn made that Bobby had told her that the C.I.A. took part in the assassination of Dominicam Republic President Raphael Trujillo—plus other incriminating records of the things Bobby Kennedy had told her.

Why did Marilyn keep this diary? She told my client that after a couple of dates with Bobby Kennedy, who was then Attorney General of the United States and brother of the President, that he (Bobby) chastised her for *not* remembering certain things he had previously told her. Sometimes he would give her an update on certain work he was doing—so she went to a stationery store and bought a red diary for the purpose of keeping notes on what Bobby Kennedy had told her. Her entries were not kept on a daily basis, for Marilyn was not a diary-keeper. She only made notes after she left meetings with Bobby Kennedy, and kept them in chronological order. Prior to each time she would see Bobby, she would get out her diary—which she cautiously kept guarded in her large purse—and review what he had told her the time before.

This kept her, as she said, on "top of things," and they got along much better after that, although all of the information Bobby Kennedy was telling her, either out of trying to impress her with his work or was through loose and careless talk, involved *serious* national security at the time.

Marilyn further told Slatzer, when he asked *why* Bobby Kennedy dwelled on talking about his work so much, that unlike JFK, who mesmerized her with the discussion of literature, paintings, sailing, and the nice things in life that interested her much more, Bobby just boasted about *who* he was going after in his fight against crime plus the hard work he was doing to accomplish certain things through his position "regardless as to how I do it."

Marilyn, who had nothing more than a tenth grade education, with a "C" average in most of her high school courses, was far from being a political science student. In fact, she herself questioned many of the entries that she wrote in her diary as she did not know what they meant. But being an actress, with memory an asset, she recorded classified government information that obviously led to her murder.

The private phone number Bobby had given her, which he answered personally, was disconnected less that twenty-four hours after she had naively mentioned to him that she had been keeping a diary of "all of the things" he told her that last summer of her life in 1962. It has been theorized that this red diary became her "ace in the hole" against Bobby Kennedy after his sudden cut-off of *all* communications with her just ten days before her body was discovered. After all, less than twenty-four hours before she died (and it has been established that she had been dead since about 8:00 p.m. the night of August 4, 1962) she told my client, that unless she heard from Bobby Kennedy over the weekend she was going to hold a news conference on Monday morning, August 6, 1962, and "blow the lid off this whole damned thing."

By that, Marilyn implied that she was going to divulge openly to the press her long-running "affair" with John F. Kennedy when he was both senator and President, her affair with Bobby Kennedy in June and July of 1962, and even the red diary and its contents. She was also going to announce her new plans for the future as well.

We have nothing else to believe other than her red diary was a "walking time-bomb." She told Slatzer, when he advised her to get rid of it, that it just "might explode into the wrong faces." The explosion, unfortunately, was her murder.

Our press conference was rewarding. Many tips, leads, and bits of information were received—some of little or no value, others worthy of checking out. At least, we beat "City Hall." Bob and I felt we were responsible, after twenty years of effort on his part, and a decade on mine, for the district attorney's official re-opening of the case. For the moment, we were victorious.

Two days after our press conference, John Van de Kamp, the County District Attorney of Los Angeles, and candidate for the California Attorney General's Office, announced they would review any *new* evidence. On August 10, 1982, Mike Antonovich, a member of the County Board of Supervisors, requested and received a decision that the case be re-opened.

These new official statements made news reports worldwide. But the missing diary remained the "number one news story." The "mysterious" client of the fine-arts dealer offering $100,000 for the diary was identified as Doug Villiers, who owned the Antiquarius in Beverly Hills. I was surprised that tipsters continued to call Nick Harris Detectives rather than those offering a reward ten times greater.

The "treasure hunt" for the diary is world-wide. Even my youngsters, Holly and Jannelle, have asked me if they would get the reward if they found it. Somewhere, someplace, there is a red diary, about five by seven inches, containing cryptic notes written by Marilyn. From what we know, it will *not* say "Property of Marilyn Monroe" nor will it be a day-to-day account of her life. If you find the diary, the words it will contain most often are: "Bobby said..."

The missing red diary alone is not the missing link that will prove her murder and establish her murderers, but it will be an important piece of the puzzle. You can be assured, the $10,000 offer for the diary by Nick Harris Detectives still stands. And it is no publicity stunt—for after we see its contents, and photograph them, we plan to turn the book over to the Los Angeles County District Attorney's Office.

The diary Ted Jordan claims to have is not the diary we are seeking. There is more about Jordan and his "diary" in chapter twenty-one, "Tales of Bizarre Tipsters."

Marilyn's diary is an important link in establishing why she was murdered. More important are the clandestine tape recordings made in the Monroe home the night she died.

X

Bernard Spindel,

A Legend In His Own Time

Bernard Bates Spindel was without question the "King" of the wiretappers. His notoriety in this particular electronic field made him a legend in his own time. He was extremely respected by his peers as well as his adversaries. Those persons who were very close to him, whom he considered friends, were allowed to call him "Bernie." Jimmy Hoffa was his principal client during the 1950s and 1960s, but Bernie never considered him a friend, just a client.

Spindel was multi-faceted, a specialist in his field, a man without a college degree who obtained his vast knowledge by electronic eavesdropping which would make him famous throughout the world. His early training in wiretapping began while serving a tour of duty with the United States Army Signal Corps. There he mastered the art of bugging, and in later years would outclass his instructors. And from there, he was assigned as an intelligence officer until the end of World War II.

After he had finished his military hitch, he made an application to join the Central Intelligence Agency. He would have been an excellent candidate, but the official records show he was turned down. Therefore, Bernie decided to open his own detective bureau. His agency apparently became a front for his electronic surveillance activities.

Spindel was married to Barbara Fox. They had six children. After his death on February 2, 1971, it was reported that two of them attempted suicide. But for reasons known only to the family, everything was kept in his wife's name, even the company, which carried the title of B.R. Fox Company.

In 1968 he took time out of his busy life to write a book entitled, *The Ominous Ear*. In it he wrote, "When a citizen does it [taps a phone], it's wiretapping. For the FBI, it's called monitoring. The telephone company calls it, 'observing.'" Although the book was far from a best-seller, because it was what publishing houses would call a "specialty book," it was very informative. (My own first manuscript several years ago was titled, *Shhh!*, and it concerned the matter of privacy invasion and how to prevent it. Somehow it just never found a publisher. I think the public then was quite more interested in learning about how it was done, rather than how to prevent it.)

But Bernie Spindel was more than just a wiretapper. As a matter of record, he was also responsible for detecting and retrieving illegal taps. Among his many accomplishments was serving as a technical advisor for an ad hoc citizens' organization called the New York City Anti-Crime Commission. Many important names were among members who established this commission to fight police corruption in New York.

There was a considerable amount of mystique about Spindel, who was known to be quite a "loner," But even

those close to him did not really know who he really
pledged his allegiance to. Some thought of him only as
Jimmy Hoffa's man, others as a Mafia wire man. Bernie
was even thought to belong to the C.I.A., an agency that
had earlier rejected his talents. His widow still believes
that he was some sort of a government agent. After his
death, she learned he was eligible for a military funeral,
but she was advised to bury him in a private cemetery so
as "not to cause embarrassment" for certain organizations
and persons.

As far back as July 1959, Bernie Spindel had
encountered Bobby Kennedy face-to-face. At that
particular time, he had a counter-intelligence job against
the McClellan Investigation Committee On Labor
Racketeering, before which Spindel had appeared.
Following a hearing one day, Spindel met Kennedy in the
hallway of the Senate Office Building and asked him if the
rumor he had heard was true that Kennedy had forwarded
a file on Spindel to the Internal Revenue Service for
further study.

Kennedy admitted that he had and added, "I hope they
get you. They're certainly going to try." Just a few
months prior, in the spring of 1959, Bobby Kennedy had
sent a staff investigator, James P. Kelly, to invite Spindel
to meet with him (Kennedy) on a certain Sunday afternoon
at the Park Avenue apartment of the Kennedy family. Now
Spindel had known Kelly prior to his having joined the
staff of the McClellan Committee when he had been a
narcotics detective with the New York Police Department
and Spindel was with the Anti-Crime Committee.
Although Spindel had agreed to the meeting, there was
actually no business conducted at the apartment, because
both Kennedy and Kelly had to leave for the airport, and
Spindel agreed to drive them in his car. Unknown to
Kennedy, a transcript of the recorded conversation that
took place en route to the airport reveals Robert

Kennedy's eagerness to "get something on Jimmy Hoffa."

In fact, Bobby Kennedy wanted Spindel to testify against Hoffa. But Spindel refused and tried to joke his way out of it by suggesting that a loan of $850,000 be set up for him to establish an electronics firm in Puerto Rico. Bobby Kennedy didn't quite take this as a joke, and he countered with a statement that Spindel found quite shocking. He said, "If you testify to what I want you to...my brother will be the next President of the United States and you can have anything you like."

More than six years would pass before this conversation would be confirmed in court by sworn testimony. Spindel never quite intended to be a double agent, when he was subpoenaed by the Senate to testify against James Hoffa in a summons dated July 15, 1959. Of course Bobby Kennedy knew that Spindel would not testify, but instead put on the stand Carmino Bellino, who was an accountant for the committee. Bellino placed into the record his account of what had been told him regarding Spindel's finances. This was on page 19828 of the transcript of the McClellan hearings and reads as follows:

> CHAIRMAN McCLELLAN: You have heard these statements. Is there anything inaccurate in the testimony by Mr. Bellino, Mr. Spindel?
> MR. SPINDEL: There are many inaccuracies, but at this time I choose not to make any statement and assert my rights under the Fifth Amendment. I would like to make, if the Chairman is really interested in finding out the facts, I would like to make a statement pertaining to the Chief Counsel of the Committee.
> THE CHAIRMAN: That is what you were called here for, Sir. If you are going to take the Fifth Amendment—any statement you want to make criticizing the people on this committee...
> MR. SPINDEL: I am not criticizing it. If you were

interested in facts, these facts are what the
Committee ought to have.

THE CHAIRMAN: You will have to make them
somewhere else.

MR. SPINDEL: I certainly will. [At this point, Bobby
Kennedy said the following:]

BOBBY KENNEDY: I have had some conversation
with Mr. Spindel. Mr. Spindel wanted material that
we had obtained from him kept confidential. I had
some conversation with him along these lines. After
he had given me the information, he wanted to have
my agreement that it would be kept confidential. At
that time, of course, I wanted him to testify. He
made a statement to me at that time that it would be
possible that he would consider testifying if it
would be possible for me to make arrangements to
have him set up business in Puerto Rico.

MR. SPINDEL: That is an absolute lie and he knows
that.

BOBBY KENNEDY: It would not have to be handled
directly, Mr. Chairman; it could be handled
indirectly.

THE CHAIRMAN: Let us not go into this now. If we
are going to do that, this witness will have the right
to make a statement.

MR. SPINDEL: I think I should have the right to
make a statement.

THE CHAIRMAN: The Chair will hold, unless you
can testify on the things we inquire about, that you
can't make any statement.

When the hearing was finally over, and Spindel stepped
out of the hearing room, he started to walk away from the
door of the committee room. Suddenly, Carmino Bellino
came charging at him, his fists clenched. Somebody yelled
for Spindel to "look out!" Spindel turned around and
Bellino swung at him, but Spindel landed a good one on
Bellino. But the bottom line was the front page of the
Washington *Daily News*, on Wednesday, July 15, 1959,

which showed a picture of James Hoffa arguing with Bobby Kennedy. The headline read: "KENNEDY DENIES WITNESS'S CLAIM OF JOB OFFER TO TESTIFY AGAINST HOFFA."

However, Spindel was well ahead of them because in his briefcase he had brought along the recording of the conversation that he had made in the car as well as a typewritten transcript. After this, that aspect of the particular incident somehow died very, very quickly. And Robert Kennedy had predicted, his brother JFK was going to be the next President of the United States. And Robert Kennedy was appointed United States Attorney General. And that's when the heat began to be on for both Spindel and Hoffa.

I would like to repeat here that Spindel never intended to be a double agent, even when he was subpoenaed to testify against Hoffa. The $850,000 "loan" was never received. I think Bernie knew that if he crossed Hoffa he would be a dead man, and besides, my investigation revealed that Spindel was extremely loyal to his clients, regardless of who they were. I really believe that Spindel knew his time on earth would be a short one, because since childhood, he had suffered both a heart and a thyroid condition, which did eventually take his life. He lived very well, however, having a large house, a beautiful pool, and luxurious automobiles at his home in Holmes, New York.

The "King" of the wiretappers enjoyed his reputation. Not only did he "bug" phones and rooms, he even taped the F.B.I. car-to-car radio transmissions. After Hoffa's conviction on charges of jury-tampering in Nashville, the F.B.I. placed five of Hoffa's closest associates under surveillance. One of them was Spindel. The Bureau's interest was primarily *when* Hoffa would be with one of the five.

The following "bugged" FBI surveillance team's

transmission later became part of the trial record. It went as follows:

> "Say, Bill, the two occupants with the man [Jimmy Hoffa] and the ex-boxer [Chuck O'Brien, a Teamster business agent]."
>
> "That's a 10-4-correct. Is the car parked on the 11th Street side?"
>
> "That's confirmed. The light beige Chevrolet right there in front of the hotel, is that a 10-4?"
>
> "That's a 10-4, Bill, Nashville tag."
>
> "23, are you trying to transmit me?"
>
> "Not me, Chief."
>
> "What's all that noise?"
>
> "I think we're tuned in."
>
> "That's probably Bernard."
>
> "Hi-ya, Boinie..."
>
> "Ha, ha, maybe there *is* a hanky-panky, huh?"
>
> "Could be."
>
> "Hi-ya, Boinie. Doing fine. Making lots of money. Working for Mr. H.? He's a good boy."
>
> "Go home, Bernard."

If all of Bernard Spindel's tapes could be transcribed, we would find not only comedy but tragedy. Like the "death tapes" of Marilyn Monroe, most of the secrets that Spindel learned from his bugging were not shared even with his wife. But one thing we do know is that he had picked up information that proved Marilyn Monroe was *murdered*.

Barbara Spindel has stated that her husband was framed by the United States Department of Justice and that his imprisonment killed him. Maybe she was right. Because in 1969, Spindel was convicted for "conspiring to provide technical information about electronic eavesdropping techniques." He was convicted by a technicality, because somebody wanted to get him—and they did.

In researching this case, I discovered that Spindel was called in as a consultant for a private investigation firm that was employed by Huntington Hartford, the heir of the A & P grocery chain. Apparently he wanted to bug his wife for divorce information. Spindel himself placed no taps, just gave his colleagues technical advice. The Hartford bugging was discovered and arrests were made. None of the actual wiretappers went to jail; only the consultant Spindel was arrested and convicted. Eventually, he was sentenced to Sing-Sing Prison. Barbara Spindel would later say that the prison authorities offered to release her husband if he would talk about something to do with Bobby Kennedy, but exactly what, she did not know. Perhaps it was his knowledge of the Kennedy-Monroe tapes that he had made for Jimmy Hoffa, when he actually was eavesdropping on Bobby Kennedy but picked up the information about Marilyn Monroe quite accidentally.

Spindel was a doomed man. After eighteen months in prison, he was paroled, not for good behavior, but because he was about to die. What about the Marilyn Monroe - Bobby Kennedy tapes? Some believe that Spindel, while he made copies, which he was known to do, delivered the original to Edward Bennett Williams, Hoffa's attorney. Williams later would become the president of the Washington Redskins football team. Among Williams' other clients were Robert Vesco, Senator Joseph McCarthy, gangster Frank Costello, John Connally, Bobby Baker and the former C.I.A. director, Richard Helms. Hoffa's legal counsel successfully argued for an acquittal on bribery charges by a staffer on the McClellan Committee in late 1962, about the time of Marilyn's death. The attorney-client relationship soon ended after a heated disagreement.

After Bobby Kennedy's assassination on the night of June 5, 1968, I learned that Williams persuaded the late senator's executive secretary to become his own personal secretary. She was not only loyal to Bobby Kennedy but a close confidante. I wondered why she would want to work for the man who once represented her former boss' mortal enemy.

Apparently Spindel had made several copies of the Monroe-Kennedy tapes. Barbara Spindel reportedly said that Williams received the original, but he never made it public. Williams is *not* Mr. M., the Washington, D.C., attorney my source told me has the tapes, which we will discuss later.

The legend of Bernard Spindel lives on. If what I was told is true, he bugged the most sensational murder case ever to be recorded on tape, for a client who in his own right was also a legend and died before his time. It is quite obvious that Bernard Spindel took many secrets to his grave.

But the legend he left behind—the tapes which contain the voices talking about Marilyn Monroe's death, and phrases such as "what are we going to do with the body?"—has remained for posterity forever. Perhaps these tapes, when they surface and come to light, will be the *real* legacy that Bernard Spindel left behind.

XI

The Telltale Tapes

Marilyn Monroe was definitely not alone during the final minutes of her life. She actually was entertaining two very close and trusted friends. The two had been in her Brentwood home many times before. Soon after their work had been done, and Marilyn's spirit had left her dead body, they would leave together and plant themselves in a place where their alibis could be established.

After I had pondered over the clues that had come across my desk for the past ten years, luck came my way in the form of a very reliable informant who stated to me that her killers were not from the C.I.A., the Mafia, or any other group which had been suspected through the years. In fact, my informant told me that the names of the killers were household names known to the general public and that their voices could be easily recognized by almost anyone.

My informant, whom I talked with in August 1982, exactly twenty years after Marilyn had been found dead in her bedroom, displayed extreme sincerity as he explained a few things to me that made chills run up and down my spine.

"I was involved in something in the past that you are receiving a lot of notoriety on," he told me. "I have some information that just might help you."

Although he was what we would refer to as a "hearsay" witness, not unlike Watergate's famous "Deep Throat," he did not give me any riddles to solve. I knew he was shooting straight from the hip for he proceeded to direct me right to the source.

He made it very clear that I was never to use his name when contacting his source. My tipster shall be identified here as "Tom." That is not his real name. He did identify himself, and I promised to keep his identitiy secret. Today, protection is his business, for he is the vice-president of a large security firm. He knows full well that his past could easily damage his reputation.

"Have you ever heard of Bernard Spindel?" he asked.

"He was one of the best wiretappers in the country," I replied.

"He was the best," Tom said.

I couldn't question that, for Bernard Spindel was well-known for his longtime career in the field of electronic eavesdropping. He had bugged the F.B.I. and Bobby Kennedy for James Hoffa, scourged many police departments, fought with both Bell Telephone and the Internal Revenue Service, and become the first American to make Dominican dictator Trujillo's "execution list." His name had figured into the now-famous Marilyn Monroe tapes from a tap that his organization had allegedly placed in Marilyn's Brentwood home. Yes, I knew Spindel's work quite well.

But how did my new informant Tom fit in with Spindel? He told me that he had been a "key man" in Spindel's organization, employed by B.R. Fox, the name used for

Spindel's clandestine eavesdropping firm. Tom went over his whole background with me and I discovered he was actually an electronics engineer, responsible for designing many of Spindel's 'bugs." Then we got down to the case of Marilyn Monroe.

"Marilyn's phones were definitely tapped," he told me. "So were all the rooms of her house."

This confirmed what Bob Slatzer and I had known for years. We also had knowledge of a phone call recorded the night of her death, when someone from San Francisco asked a person in Marilyn's house—over her private phone, GR 6-1890—"Is she dead yet?" I might add that although a tap on a phone does not normally reveal the city from which the call is placed, back in 1962 long-distance calls in California had to be placed through an operator for there was no direct dialing. An operator's voice had been picked up saying the call was from San Francisco.

Bernard Spindel even admitted to my client that Marilyn's residence had been bugged. But this did not come to light until the morning of December 16, 1966, when at 3:10 a.m. a caravan of marked and unmarked State Police cars pulled into the driveway of Spindel's home in Holmes, New York. The raid was ordered by New York County District Attorney, Frank Hogan—although it was out of his jurisdiction, according to Spindel.

With this team of agents was the assistant district attorney of Putnam County; Herman Richard Zapf, chief investigator for the New York Telephone Company; and William Bechtel, Zapf's superior. Through the locked front door, Investigator Carmine Palombo of the New York State Police announced that he had a warrant for Spindel's arrest and a search warrant for the premises. Spindel asked him to show him the warrants through the glass window or insert them under the door so he could make sure they were valid. The officer refused, but

Spindel persuaded him to submit the warrants after he grabbed a 12-gauge shotgun.

Spindel read the warrants and then opened the door. The team of police quickly filed through the door while Spindel frantically dialed the number of his lawyer. During this time, Spindel's wife collapsed and a doctor was summoned to the scene immediately while Spindel's electronics laboratory was being torn apart. When the doctor arrived, he discovered that Mrs. Spindel had suffered a serious heart attack. She was taken to the hospital where it was diagnosed that she was left with permanent cardiac damage.

Spindel was arraigned before the Honorable Behrend Goosen, Justice of the Peace, Town of Southeast. The charge was that Spindel "feloniously, wrongfully, wilfully, unlawfully, and knowingly concealed and withheld and aided in concealing and withholding certain property belonging to the New York Telephone Company." However, Spindel in his trial provided the courts with paid bills for all such equipment that he had legally purchased over the past several years. A short time later, Spindel filed a million-and-a-half-dollar lawsuit against the New York Telephone Company and the State Police.

Meanwhile, an interesting story about the bugging raid on Spindel's home made a three-column story in the *New York Times* on December 21, 1966. Written by reporter Robert E. Tomasson, it read in part as follows:

SUIT ASKS RETURN OF BUGGING ITEMS
Tapes on Marilyn Monroe and others are listed

In an affidavit submitted to the court, Bernard Spindel asserted that some of the seized material contained tapes and evidence concerning the circumstances surrounding the death of Marilyn Monroe, which strongly suggests that the officially reported circumstances of her demise were erroneous.

Spindel had also upstaged the raiders by having secreted in the walls of his laboratory a tape machine that when voice-actuated would record all conversations and noises for five hours. Perhaps it was the first time in the history of wiretapping that an actual raid had been recorded. But what was most unusual, when Spindel played the tape later after he was released on bond from jail, was the conversation on the tape. He heard different voices asking each other, "What do the Marilyn Monroe tapes have to do with Bobby Kennedy?"

That incriminating tape still exists. Spindel's case was thrown out and he never did get back his tapes. After he died at the age of 45, his wife again petitioned the courts for the return of the tapes. She was told that they might have been destroyed.

When Bob Slatzer talked with Frank Hogan a few years later in New York, asking to hear some of the tapes, Hogan told him that "All of those tapes were either lost or thrown out."

But now there was a light at the end of the tunnel as my new friend Tom, described in detail *how* the bugging was actually done in those days.

"We used the lower aircraft band, 112-115 mg.," Tom explained. "It was a clear band, not monitored, seldom used."

As he continued to explain, I realized more and more that Spindel's people were real pros. For over two decades, I had been proficient in the art of counter-measures, detecting illegal wiretaps and bugs. In 1975 I gave pertinent testimony to the Presidential and Congressional National Wiretap Commission, which helped bring about some new federal laws on the subject. But Spindel's techniques were far more sophisticated in the early 1960s, for the bugs that were used to capture the voices of Marilyn's killers were smaller than books of matches.

121

The bug planted in this instance was not a crystal frequency, the kind often used during that era, but a VOX, a new technique at the time that was voice-activated and capable of starting and stopping the recorder when there were no audible sounds or voices. This saved reels of blank tape, not to mention the elimination of hours of monitoring time.

Marilyn was correct when she suspected her phones were tapped. "Bob," she had told my client, "I think someone is listening to my phone calls."

During her final days, Slatzer observed that she appeared to be very nervous and was becoming more and more suspicious of the persons around her. Yet she did not suspect that her bedroom, like all other rooms of her house, was bugged—and neither did her killers.

I asked Tom why his source, the man I shall identify as "Mr. M" had kept the tapes all these years.

"He wanted to protect Bernie," Tom replied.

Spindel had been dead for quite some time. As I later analyzed this, the only logical reason I could think of was that somehow "Mr. M" was also protecting himself by being the custodian of these incriminating tapes.

Yet, if "Mr. M" had the tapes, he would be literally walking a very dangerous tightrope—and if someone were to cut that rope, what then? I also wondered how Tom knew about the tape recording of Marilyn's last hours on this planet. His only explanation was that he had only discovered the existence of the tapes several years after Marilyn's death.

I learned that both Tom and "Mr. M" shared a common interest: both were key members in the Spindel organization, high-ranking officials. In addition to the conventional bugging, both were involved in manufacturing assassination devices for the C.I.A. They also instructed local and federal law enforcement agents on bugging and debugging. "Mr. M" still does. They had shared a very close personal relationship, a very trusting one, quite confidential on a business basis, Tom revealed to me.

"Forget that red diary, Milo, get the tapes," Tom said sharply. He mentioned something about "shoptalk" between himself and "Mr. M" and I asked him what that was all about.

"Marilyn was slapped around," he began. "You could actually hear her being slapped, even hear her body fall to the floor. You could hear her hit the deck, and all the sounds that took place in her house that night..."

Now the pieces were beginning to fit together.

As his description wound up, he concluded, "And one of them actually said, 'What do we do with her body now?'—words to that effect. I remember there was some concern over where to put her body or something like that. It's all on the tape."

All the facts added up to one thing: there definitely was a cover-up, and a few persons close to Marilyn were lying through their teeth.

Over the years I had been engaged to work on many cases in which suicide was alleged but the victim was actually murdered. Some cases were just the opposite. But I do recall one case in particular, just after Marilyn's mysterious death, when I was retained to investigate a man accused of murdering his wife. He claimed that she had committed suicide. My client was a noted California attorney, who had been retained to defend him, and after my detailed preliminary investigation, I told him that I felt his client was guilty.

The death scene, much like Marilyn's, had been conveniently rearranged, appearing to indicate suicide. But one important clue was overlooked: the victim was *left*-handed, and she had supposedly slashed her wrist with her *right* hand. Dr. Thomas Noguchi had performed the autopsy. It was this case that brought me together with Dr. Noguchi for the first time.

The investigation showed reasonable doubt. But when the case went to court, the jury delivered their verdict that the husband was innocent of murder. After the trial, the defendant said to me: "Milo, if I told you I killed her, what would happen?"

He knew that he could not be tried again for the same crime for he was protected by the double jeopardy law. It was just the case of an innocent female being killed by her husband, who made it appear a suicide and who came out smelling like a rose.

Through the years, no one has ever confessed to murdering Marilyn Monroe. Or have they? Those voices on the Spindel tapes are the real confession. During our investigation, we had reliable sources that verified our information who really ordered the "bugs" for Marilyn's house and phones. But I wanted to hear it directly from Tom's lips.

"Bernie Spindel was Jimmie Hoffa's personal man," Tom told me, "And you had better believe he had a good tap on her house."

"And you can say that in all truthfulness?" I asked.

"I tell you it's a fact right now," Tom insisted, sticking to his story. "The tapes will tell you everything you want to hear and maybe a little bit more. The hell with the diary. The tapes are what you really want, for the voices of the killers are right there."

Tom confirmed my theory as we talked awhile longer. The major mystery my informant had *solved*, through his scenario, was the exact identity of Marilyn's two killers. It was not difficult for me to believe him after all of this interrogation. He was for real.

He went on to explain how Spindel had died in a New York prison in the early seventies at the age of 45. The New York police ascribed his death to a fatal heart attack. That was questionable, too. But even after Spindel's death, he told me that their work continued.

"We had a lab in Alexandria, Virginia," he added, "and two fronts were created: one in the Watergate complex and the second one was off Pennsylvania Avenue right near the White House—and we were cooking at full steam."

I felt it to be somewhat ironic when he mentioned the Watergate location.

More ironic is the fact that the source, "Mr. M," the man man who had the murder tapes, now has offices in the Watergate complex. I learned that he is a practicing attorney, well respected, who closely guards any conversation that involves his former relationship with Spindel.

As soon as I learned the true identity of Marilyn's killers and "Mr. M," I realized that I too would be walking that treacherous tightrope, and most certainly did not want to fall. I made secret contacts with highly placed persons throughout the nation, disclosing this knowledge for my own protection.

I allowed the news to leak to the media that I was on the track of Marilyn's *death tapes*. I hoped this would help smoke out the tapes. Originally, I intended to turn all of this information over to the Los Angeles County District Attorney's office, but I was talked out of it by a veteran newspaper reporter with the New York *Post*.

"Give it to George Carpozi," he told me. He further explained that this way I would not have to identify my source. Carpozi, also a veteran news reporter on the New York *Post*, was already hot on the Marilyn story and had written six full-page stories that ran that many consecutive days in the *Post*, stirring up the murder of Marilyn Monroe on the twentieth anniversay of her death.

I finally agreed to go along with the *Post*. I would be credited if the tapes were recovered. However, I insisted that they be given to the Los Angeles County District Attorney's office. Then Carpozi and I got down to brass tacks.

"Carpozi," I said, "we have two things to offer 'Mr. M,': anonymity and money, both of which I know the *Post* can arrange."

The deal was welded together and we decided to go in this direction.

Carpozi called "Mr. M" from his office in New York City and said he wanted to talk about the Marilyn Monroe tapes.

"I don't speak to anybody about the tapes on the phone," he told Carpozi.

He did agree to meet in Washington, D.C. Unfortunately, we could not use Tom's name. Now I began to feel uneasy about the contact being made. But I felt that if "Mr. M" did not want to talk, he could have very easily hung up the phone on Carpozi and not agreed to a meeting in Washington.

"Mr. M" and Carpozi talked over a two-day period. "Mr. M" confirmed one fact to Carpozi: there was a definite relationship between Marilyn and one of the persons my tipster had said was one of Marilyn's murderers.

But "Mr. M" flatly denied to Carpozi having the tapes, adding that he would not even admit to hearing them. He was, in fact, calling my informant a liar, yet he never knew who tipped us to him. I was later displeased to learn that the New York *Post* did not offer to protect "Mr. M's" name nor did they offer to buy the tapes, which I felt could have been accomplished. As a result, Carpozi went back home "tapeless."

I still was confident that the tapes would surface. "Mr. M" had good reason for denying any knowledge of them. He had no guarantee that his name would be kept out of the case, and he had nothing to gain financially by going through all this hassle. All he could possibly expect was that somebody might just shake the tightrope he carefully walked, and he could end up sharing Marilyn's fate.

My tipster, Tom, in my own professional opinion, was honest and sincere. Without the Spindel/Hoffa tapes, it would be unethical for me to reveal the true identities of the *killers*. All of us who share this knowledge have agreed to keep it secret. But this much I can say: one of Marilyn's killers is still alive. He was one of the two men in her house the night she died, and she invited them there, knowing both of them quite well. One was a high-ranking political appointee. His feet often walked over the carpeting of the White House. The other is a well-known star of motion pictures.

One thing I believe: several copies of Marilyn's death tapes were made. When the publicity diminishes—soon, I hope—I would not at all be surprised to receive a package with no return address, containing the tapes. I will send them to a voice print laboratory, and they will be tested with a new scientific tool that can identify voices just like fingerprints.

If my informant was right, these tapes will prove who murdered Marilyn Monroe. We do know, through our long investigation, that there was a massive cover-up. It would have to have involved many persons, and perhaps as I once disclosed "a dissident-type faction of the C.I.A. or a similar governmental agency."

I for one do not like being tagged as subscribing to a conspiracy theory; but professionally, in this case, regardless of who killed her, I know that there was a very clever and clandestine cover-up.

She did not—and could not—take her life as has been reported in the media of the world for the past two decades. Now I believe we know the real identities of her killers and we are closer now than ever before to revealing those names to the world. When those tapes are played, it

will be a devastating shock to all who hear them.
And that time is not too far away.

MARILYN...in pictures.

Most are previously unpublished

Norma Jeane Mortensen, seven months old.
One of her first portraits.

*Norma Jeane, age two, with her mother at
the Santa Monica Beach in California.*

Age four.

Age twelve.

1953

1957

1962

Marilyn Monroe in 1951.

The following photographs were taken from Marylin's last movies, **Something's Got to Give**, *which never was released.*

Marilyn with Bob Slatzer in 1950.

Bobby Kennedy.

Eunice Murray, Marilyn's housekeeper-companion.

Rare photo of Dr. Ralph Greenson, Marilyn's last psychiatrist.

Dr. Hyman Engelberg, Marilyn's doctor.

Sergeant Jack Clemmons, first police officer to arrive on the scene. he thought Marilyn was murdered.

Rare photo of Pat Newcomb, Marilyn's Press Agent.

Lionel Grandison, Deputy Coroner's Aide, forced to sign Marilyn Monroe's death certificate.

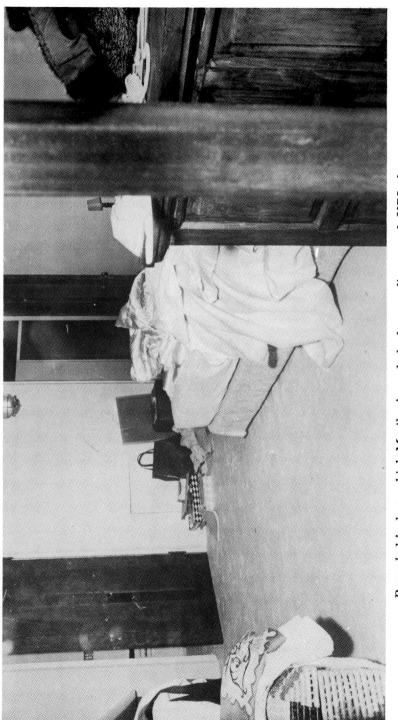

Rumpled bed on which Marilyn's nude body was discovered. UPI photo.

Marilyn's body released by the Los Angeles Coroner to the Westwood Mortuary. UPI photo.

XII

The Secret Meeting on the 18th Floor

"I demand an official investigation into the death of Marilyn Monroe," I announced at one of the largest news conferences in the history of the Greater Los Angeles Press Club on August 4, 1982.

For years, my client and I endeavored to get an official investigation. In 1974, we petitioned the Los Angeles County Grand Jury for an investigation into the strange death of Marilyn Monroe. As most people know, the Grand Jury changes from year to year. But that particular year, when we supplied them with massive evidence, which had been built up over a period of a dozen years, a letter came back containing one paragraph. It read to the effect that their opinion of what they had evaluated did not merit the reopening of the case. The persons who investigated the case originally were said to be competent and complete in their findings, according to the Foreman of the 1974 Los Angeles County Grand Jury.

Another year passed. In 1975, armed with a little more

information and even further clarifying the details contained in the 1974 request, we took the same tack. Since there was a new Grand Jury that year, we hoped that we would be heard and that we would not be a voice in the wilderness as we had been for the past thirteen years. It was only a matter of three or four weeks before a reply came back that was very similar to the one in 1974. It seemed like a useless endeavor to try and enlist the help of anyone of the annual Grand Juries. They would not review the case, much less reopen it.

The only other alternative was to direct a demand to the coroner's office, namely to Coroner Thomas Noguchi. After we discussed this, and especially in light of the fact that Dr. Noguchi had been criticized by some other medical authorities and some reporters for the way he had handled the Marilyn Monroe case, we decided that this too would obviously be in vain. Where else would we go? The only other answer was to the Los Angeles County District Attorney. And we soon found that that door was closed to us, too.

In 1975, Bob Slatzer was guest on the weekly Sam Yorty Show, which was telecast every Sunday evening at prime time over KCOP-TV, Channel 13 in Los Angeles. The show was taped in advance Friday afternoon. When Slatzer arrived at the television station, he did not know who was going to be on the show with him. That information is seldom told to a guest. There isn't any particular reason for this, except that it really doesn't matter and therefore there usually isn't any reason for one guest to ask the producer who else is going to be on the show.

However, in this case, my client was sitting in the make-up room of the studio when Joe Bush, Los Angeles County District Attorney, strolled in, sat down and waited to be made up for the show. Now Slatzer and Bush, two men who were obviously of different opinions over the death of Marilyn Monroe, were sitting side by side. Slatzer had told

Bush about the two requests, which Bush acknowledged knowing about, even the recent one just of a few weeks before. Slatzer had asked him why he would not open the case, or at least review it. After all, there had not been any coroner's inquest, and although that is not always a necessity, there were a few hundred reporters around the world who had written about it, thinking that it should have been done in the case of Marilyn Monroe.

Joe Bush smiled, leaned back in his chair, looked at Slatzer, and said "As long as I'm District Attorney, that case will never be opened."

No sooner had Bush made that remark than Sam Yorty was seen looming in the doorway, smiling. The former mayor of Los Angeles sat down in the third make-up chair, saying to Bush, "Aw, c'mon, Joe, why don't you open up that case? A lot of people have been wondering why it's been such a secret."

Joe Bush just looked at Sam and changed the subject, and then the make-up girl came in and went over to Yorty and started making him up, and that terminated the conversation.

For some reason, Joe Bush was not interested in opening up the Marilyn Monroe case at all. To him, as he was later to comment to Slatzer when my client pushed him again about it before he left the show, Joe Bush just said politely, "It's a closed door."

Why then, did John Van de Kamp, District Attorney of Los Angeles County, agree to open the case and conduct an investigation? I had previously planned to make such a demand on the twentieth anniversary of Marilyn Monroe's death. I never realized that there would be so much media attention focused on this particular anniversary, compared to others, which had just had a little bit of television coverage and print in various papers for one or two days at the most. But for some uncanny reason, there was a tremendous surge of media attention directed toward the twentieth anniversary of the death of Marilyn Monroe.

Coincidentally, my press conference had previously been scheduled and I had already firmed up the answers and also some of the questions that I was going to feed an eager press. I felt that the claims I would make regarding her "murder" also demanded an official answer. One other point, which I felt might be a hindrance at the time, was the fact that John Van de Kamp was a candidate for the office of State Attorney General, with the election coming up the first week of November 1982. I felt that it probably was a little unfair to make such a demand when such a reputable man was running for office, but again the timing was quite coincidental.

After I had announced my request to the media, the word got around, said to have originated in the Los Angeles County District Attorney's office, that I was doing all of this for publicity. That was not true. It did not take the people downtown very long to learn that was not the case; and those involved, investigating me, determined that I was "quite credible" and further, that I was dealing with an extremely serious matter, which I am extremely serious about solving. What some of the people who obviously drew foredrawn conclusions did not know was that this happened to be the longest-running case in the career of Nick Harris Detectives. And after spending ten years of time checking out everything from wild goose chases to some authentic evidence, and the expense of travel, telephone, secretarial help and everything that accompanied such an investigation, I certainly was not doing this for the publicity.

Once my credibility had been established (which nobody had ever questioned before), an open communication between my office and that of the District Attorney was established. On September 22, 1982, I called Ronald H. Carroll, better known as "Mike" Carroll, on his unlisted private telephone. Mike Carroll is the number one man, the Assistant District Attorney, second only in command to John Van de Kamp.

"Milo," he said, "did you get hold of the tapes?" He was referring to the clandestine tapes made at Marilyn's home, which quite by accident had recorded the sounds of the murder.

"Not yet," I answered, "but speaking of tapes, do you have an audio cassette tape recorder in your office?"

Mike replied that he didn't but he would certainly order one for our scheduled "secret" meeting in his office the following day.

Although I had not yet me Mike Carroll, I felt that I knew him to some extent. During the past month, our names often appeared in newspaper articles about the Marilyn Monroe case. In preparation for our meeting, I did some checking on Mike. He obviously had done quite a bit of checking on me. I know that this is something very few people do, but in my business, regardless of the position or office a person holds, it has been a habit for me to operate in this manner. And it certainly wasn't anything against the good reputation and background and excellent political career of Mike Carroll. The report came back very soon, and after reading it, I made an evaluation that he was a man I could trust.

The next afternoon I arrived for my 2:00 appointment downtown. Mike Carroll's office had arranged for me to park in their private parking lot, adjacent to the Los Angeles County Criminal Courts Building at 210 West Temple Street. As I got out of my car, I glanced at my watch and saw that it was approximately 1:50 p.m. and I was arriving a little bit early. A few minutes before 2:00, I pushed the elevator button and waited with a few other persons to take the trip upstairs.

Mike Carroll's office is located on the eighteenth floor. When I had checked the directory, I had noticed the name of Dr. Thomas Noguchi still listed as the Los Angeles County Coroner. I thought this was rather strange, since he had been demoted several months previously, and his name stood out like a sore thumb. He had played quite an important role in the case of Marilyn Monroe, and I didn't feel too comfortable that he was housed in the same building.

I waited patiently as the elevator stopped several times and then suddenly made its stop on the eighteenth floor. As I walked out of the elevator, I discovered that the Los Angeles County District Attorney and his staff occupied the entire floor. It felt good to be inside where there was some comfortable air conditioning, because on that particular day in September 1982 the temperature was over 95 degrees, and it was quite smoggy. I made a "pit stop" at the water fountain, and almost burned my lips. I didn't quite quench my thirst, but at least it was wet.

Entering any office on the eighteenth floor is impossible without an appointment. And the only way to get in is through a single reception area where the large sign by the door reads: "Law Enforcement Personnel, Wear Your Badge or Identification Card." Although I had neither, my name was what counted. Moments later, after I had been announced, I was greeted by Alan Tomich, who is one of the special investigators assigned to the County District Attorney's division. I was later to learn that Al was the chief investigator assigned to the Monroe inquiry. Earlier, I had discovered that he had already been quite overworked on this assignment, putting in close to ten hours a day. Alan introduced himself to me, we shook hands, and he led me immediately into Mike Carroll's office.

Alan presented me to Mike Carroll, and in turn I was also introduced to Clayton Anderson, who was the chief investigator for the County District Attorney's office. After the formalities were over, we all sat down. I was now in the same room with the three major officials who were in charge of the Marilyn Monroe investigation. The door closed swiftly behind us and we got down to points.

I was seated directly in front of Mike Carroll, Alan to my left, Clayton to my right. The tape recorder that I had requested was on Carroll's desk. After we discussed a few aspects of the investigation, I withdrew an audio cassette tape from the Manila envelope that I had carried with me. "The tape runs about fifteen minutes," I explained.

All of them knew that I had brought a tape for them to listen to, but what they did not know was *what* was on it. Before playing the tape, I explained its origin; that it was legally obtained, but under a very unusual method. It was agreed that no law would be broken by recording or playing this tape. After all, it held quite pertinent information that would help them unveil the murder of Marilyn Monroe.

I handed the tape to Alan, who inserted it into his Panasonic recorder, which was labeled "County of Los Angeles." He then closed the lid and pushed the play button. We sat there silently as a few feet of static filled the room. Just a few hundred feet away was the press room, where members of the media worked the County District Attorney's beat. Any one of them would have given up a months' salary, and perhaps more, to hear this tape. But that was an opportunity that they would never receive. At least from me. My loyalty now was to the people in this room. Alan even stated, as we listened for the tape to start rolling, "We are not giving anything to the press."

I had long awaited this moment. Because what they were about to hear would certainly open their ears, if not their minds. When I first heard what was on the tape, it "nearly blew my mind." Although I had heard and studied it many times, it would be the first time that these three top public officials would hear it. As the leader of the tape

151

passed, the voices revealed numerous "facts." I carefully watched the reaction of the three men. I think they felt the way I did when I first heard the tape, that the contents were extremely powerful and revealing.

I might add that the County District Attorney's office realized that I was completing a book about Marilyn's death, describing the ten-year investigation during which I had spearheaded the murder theory, and they also knew the names of the media that were hounding me for interviews. I was asked not to disclose "important" information about our "secret" meeting. I made that agreement with them. We discussed other things, after the tape had played, and I allowed Alan to photocopy several important documents I presented to them.

This much I can reveal: The tape recording was not evidence; it was information, which I considered came from a most unimpeachable source. I even had other documentation to back it up. This alone, I felt, would not be quite strong enough to demand a grand jury investigation, because the foundation, even though it appeared to be rather strong, had one missing element. The key question was, could *they* obtain the missing element?

When the meeting, which lasted for quite a while, was over, I felt that it had been most informative, and my feeling was that they also appreciated what I had to offer. When I first learned that their office was conducting an investigation into Marilyn's death, I had doubts that it would be more than cursory, and then possibly dismissed as without merit. But from my private sources, and conversations with the people in the office that day, I felt that their endeavors would be quite sincere and that they would do a very complete investigation.

I had agreed not to go public with the information that I kept in my files, and that I presented at this secret meeting on the eighteenth floor. However, in order for the

County District Attorney's office to recommend further investigation, or turn it over to the Los Angeles County Grand Jury, they will need further, absolute proof, if not a confession. Twenty years after the fact, this might be somewhat difficult—since this "murder" case is considered by the media throughout the world as the "crime of the century."

I had told Mike Carroll in our meeting that I didn't want him to think that I was doing this to sell my book on Marilyn Monroe's death, and explained that in addition to being an investigator I am also an established author. I left Mike a copy of my current book in print titled, *How To Protect Your Life And Property*, which I autographed for him. I even told him that there is a section about his office in the book, which seemed to interest him.

In this book, I had written a chapter entitled "Mr. District Attorney." It reads in part:

"...Unless [the District Attorney] is assured of a solid case, the chance for conviction, that many guilty persons...are let go and don't face trial."

As I have pointed out, the *evidence* that will lead to the conviction must be extremely solid, and it is extremely rare in any criminal proceedings that a murder committed two decades ago would *ever* be brought to trial.

Mike flipped over the back cover of my book, and after reading the copy he laid it down on his desk and smiled.

"Better not show this book to your boss, [John Van de Kamp]," I said. I made this remark only because there was a further paragraph that read:

"Violent crime is completely out of control...there is roughly a 50% chance that you or a close friend or family member will be a victim of a serious crime within the next 14 months."

The quote was from George Nicholson, Senior Assistant Attorney General of the State of California, who was a candidate for the attorney general's office, opposing Los

Angeles County District Attorney John Van de Kamp.

My final advice to the district attorney's people was, "Wiretappers seldom retrieve their bugs, it's too risky to do." I hoped they would keep that in mind during their investigation.

Editor's Note:

On November 2, 1982, John Van de Kamp was elected to the office of Attorney General of the State of California.

XIII
A Leak In The Roof

Back in 1977, an actress-nightclub entertainer by the name of Paula Lane contacted my client and told him that she had learned some interesting information regarding the fact that Marilyn's home in Brentwood had actually been "bugged." When I received the call from Slatzer, telling me the results of his findings, I made a separate file on this matter because it seemed to come from a quite authentic source. It was no new revelation that Marilyn's home was actually "bugged," as she had herself suspected and knew in those last few weeks before her death in 1962.

It seemed that Miss Lane, who had won a Marilyn Monroe look-alike contest back when Marilyn was still living, and who even today resembles Marilyn quite distinctly, had hired a man to haul some dirt away from a construction site where she was building a new home. As she related her story, when she was writing out the check to pay the man for his services, he had noticed some pictures of her on the wall of her bar, along with those of Marilyn, and had commented the close resemblance. It was then that this man, who also did various jobs such as hauling dirt, roofing, and other general handiwork, mentioned the fact that just a few months previous he had been called to a residence in Brentwood to repair a leak in the roof. While he was there, he learned that the house was the former residence of Marilyn Monroe.

Although his job was only to repair a leaking roof, he stated to Miss Lane that in doing so he had found a large amount of *wiring* and a few pieces of *other equipment*, objects that were miniature transmitters.

The discovery was made when the man was on the roof of Marilyn's home. Apparently his foot went through a certain area of the tile roof, which had been rotted away by the exposure to rain and moisture through the years, and which had to be replaced. Beneath it was a shallow crawl-space, in which he found wiring running, and some old rusted relay transmitters. He notified the current tenants of the house as to his discovery. Apparently the tenants were more interested in having the leak repaired than in worrying about finding some old wiring and what he described as "transmitters." Therefore, according to the man, he pulled all the wiring and other equipment out, and filled a small trash can about halfway.

Actress Paula Lane had transmitted most of the points of this story to Slatzer and given him the man's phone number. He called, and the roofer confirmed the story. He admitted having discovered the wiring and what he identified as old rusted relay transmitters, confirming the fact that they had been under the tiles for quite some time—in his own estimate, possibly fifteen to twenty years. When questioned as to how he could identify such equipment, being in the occupation that he was in, he had mentioned the fact that he was familiar with electronic eavesdropping equipment when he was with Military Intelligence. Although we never saw the wiring that was pulled and thrown out, along with the other electronic devices, we had this man's word for it.

It is quite evident, from the information I have gathered, that Marilyn Monroe had reason to believe that her telephones had been "tapped" that summer of 1962. However, what she perhaps did not know was that a few rooms of her home were actually "bugged" as well. Add to that the fact that most of her last phone calls to Bob Slatzer were conducted through pay telephones, for which Marilyn carried around almost a pound of change in her big purse. There had been times when she had run out of change, because of the long conversations and the insertions of dozens of quarters into the pay phone, and Slatzer had told the operator to bill the rest of the charges to his personal phone number. He even told Marilyn to call him collect in the future, rather than be weighted down with carrying around a lot of change. In their last few conversations, when she called him, she reversed the charges, and he accepted. The fact that she did not call from the convenience of her home, because of her *great fear* that her telephones were "tapped," was highly significant to Slatzer, and even more so to me when I took over the case.

Perhaps even more interesting is the fact that twenty years later when Marilyn's death was being investigated by the office of the Los Angeles County District Attorney, three investigators from that office showed up at Marilyn's old home in September 1982 and asked the current owners if they could "look around." Bear in mind that this Spanish-style house has sloping ceilings, which are beamed, and has an inverted ceiling in the main living room. This does not provide much space between the outside tiles on the roof and the inside in which to plant a bug. However, there are areas where such bugs could be placed with wire running under the tile on the roof. Even back in 1962, there were also rather sophisticated "bugs" that could be placed in a room inconspicuously, and did not require any wiring.

According to the information I have assembled, the trio of investigators looking over Marilyn Monroe's old home that day were overheard expressing their doubts as to the possibility of Marilyn's home being either "bugged" (meaning the rooms) and/or "tapped" (meaning the telephones). At the time, they spent nearly two hours investigating the premises.

Then, sometime in the first week of October, one of the investigators arrived on the premises one morning accompanied by two men from General Telephone Company. Conversation was overheard by the tenants about the possibility of Marilyn's home being "wired," "telephone lines tapped," or "rooms bugged." They spent nearly an hour examining the various wires coming into the house from the telephone poles, and the one man from General Telephone even climbed to the top of a nearby telephone pole and made quite a lengthy examination. When he came down, he stated to the investigator that although there was no trace of extra wiring or bugging equipment attached to the telephone pole, which was the same pole that had stood there at the time Marilyn lived in the house, there were indications that various items had been attached to the pole and removed. So it became a question as to whether or not equipment had actually been attached to that particular pole. The telephone representative stated that it was possible, but there was no remaining tangible evidence of it left.

After this, and a lot of looking around the house, following wires and checking telephone switchboxes, they did run across a set of five multi-colored wires that emerged from the area of the guest house, running through a pipe up into the spouting alongside the garage, continuing toward the backyard, then making a complete right-angle turn to continue across the back of Marilyn's home in the spouting, and finally dipping down into the vertical section of spouting that provided the runoff for water draining from the roof of the house.

The senior representative of the telephone company was overheard saying that the wiring was quite old, possibly twenty years, and although it certainly looked like a type of wiring used by the telephone company, there was no way that General Telephone would have installed it. First of all, all of those five wires were normally enclosed in a sheath, and they most certainly would not place wiring in spoutings, covered up by leaves. They tested these wires with a special gauge to check any possible current that might be running through them, and found them to be totally *dead*. Just what were these mysterious wires, which looked so much like telephone wires that nobody would be likely to question them? Where did they come from, and who put them there?

Obviously, there had to be some motive to bring the investigative team and the representatives from the telephone company out to Marilyn's house, and they must have taken the idea of her home being "bugged" more seriously than anticipated.

Of course, I did a little investigating myself, prior to the time that the investigators from downtown appeared on the scene. The wire that was discovered in the spouting *was* multi-colored, and the gauge of it was slightly larger than that which the telephone company would use, although it certainly did resemble that particular type of wire, minus the sheath. Ordinarily, eavesdroppers use *two* wires. However, twenty years ago, a lot of unconventional things were done. Perhaps only two of these five wires actually were used, and the others were to throw off any suspicion, and to repeat, made to look like telephone wires which nobody would question. The fact that the senior telephone representative, a man obviously very knowledgeable about wiring and bugs, stated that the wiring was over twenty years old confirmed my evaluation of a small sample of the wire.

By investigating a little further, I also discovered another important fact, and that is the following: The telephone wires and their junction boxes in Marilyn Monroe's house today are in different positions and places than they were at the time Marilyn lived in that house. In fact, when Marilyn occupied that house, the wiring came directly from a distant telephone pole to a post attached to the garage. Then the wires ran down into a junction box in the garage. From what I could discover through my investigation, those mysterious wires that were so old could easily have been hooked up into the garage, although none of that wiring is evident from the inside.

A close neighbor who still lives near Marilyn's old house was questioned by one of the D.A.'s investigators, and told them that he "knew nothing" about what went on at her house. Fortunately, I was to learn through a very reliable source at Marilyn's house that the elderly gentleman confided that he had been questioned by an investigator from downtown, and had told them nothing. In fact, he stressed the idea that he knew absolutely nothing about his once-famous neighbor. That was what he told the investigator. But what he told my source is a completely different story.

He told my source that a couple of days after Marilyn's death, he had talked with Mrs. Eunice Murray, Marilyn's housekeeper-companion, and she had told him that she had left Marilyn's house in early mid-afternoon on Saturday, August 4, 1962, and that she did not return until "late that evening," at which time she discovered the "light under Marilyn's door" and that the door was "locked,"

As the years have passed, Mrs. Murray's story has varied to such an extent that if we are to believe what she originally told the police, what she reported to Slatzer, and what the neighbor claims she told him, we have quite a conflict of Mrs. Murray being in different places at the same time. It is obvious that if Mrs. Murray had left the house, as she told Slatzer, even for a few hours, we can believe the ladies at the card party when more than one of them admitted to having seen Bobby Kennedy and the man carrying the doctor's bag enter Marilyn's gates and go into her house.

If we are to recap Mrs. Murray's activities that Saturday afternoon, she first stated to the authorities, and to the press at the time, that she had not left the house but had stayed on through the night until Marilyn's body was discovered. She had also stated that Robert Kennedy had never visited Marilyn's house late that afternoon, because had he made such a visit, she would have seen him.

At this point, I think we should refer to the ladies at the card game, playing bridge, who actually saw Bobby Kennedy and another man, carrying what resembled a doctor's bag, enter Marilyn's house late that afternoon. There is definite "hard evidence" by the daughter of one of the card-playing ladies, whose mother (now deceased) was a member of the group. The daughter confirmed several years ago that this incident really happened, and that there were some very bad repercussions to the lady who owned the house, after she had mentioned this to a reporter. It was a story that was never printed. As a result, the lady owning the house where the card game took place was coerced into not telling anything to anybody by a couple of men who called upon her every other day for a few weeks, and harassed her to "keep her mouth shut," almost put her into a state of shock and aggravated her heart condition. Naturally, the woman followed the instructions.

161

If we are to believe Mrs. Murray's story that she never left the house and that if Bobby Kennedy had entered, she certainly would have seen him, she certainly contradicted herself eleven years later when she admitted to Bob Slatzer in a taped interview that she did leave the house late that afternoon for what she termed "a couple of hours or more," allegedly to go to her apartment and get some things so that she could spend the night.

Now let's go back to the elderly male neighbor, who is still living, and for reasons of his own refused to give information to the investigator from the office of the Los Angeles County District Attorney, but who confided to my source what Mrs. Murray had told him. To repeat, this was that Mrs. Murray left the house about mid-afternoon and did not return until "after dark that night," at which time she saw the "light under Marilyn's bedroom door" which was "locked."

After all, this interested the investigators from the Los Angeles County District Attorney's office enough for them to make a series of photographs showing from what vantage point one could see persons entering the gates to Marilyn's house. Add to this the statement from the elderly gentleman who still lives near Marilyn's house, and take into consideration that Mrs. Murray told him she didn't return to Marilyn's house until after dark that night, at which time she noticed the light that was on in Marilyn's bedroom. This is the part that the investigators do not know, and it is not their fault, because a lot of people are still scared to testify as to what went on the night Marilyn was found dead. My position is on the side of the investigators from the Los Angeles County District Attorney's office, and certainly my client Robert Slatzer and I have both cooperated with them. But it is my steadfast opinion that since these inconsistencies exist, in spite of the investigation they are doing, which is quite commendable, the *only way* that any of us are going to find out what *really happened* that night is to have the Los Angeles County District Attorney's office turn over its information to the grand jury, who will then call in all of these persons and make them testify under oath.

After all of this evidence has been collected, it certainly will bring the case to a point where once and for all, we will know what *really* happened.

XIV

Bobby Kennedy's "007" Briefcase

According to the syndicated columnist, Jack Anderson, Bobby Kennedy was no stranger to the bugging that went on during the Kenndy administration. On July 12, 1982, Anderson wrote: "Just prior to the New Hampshire primary, Kennedy and President Lyndon Johnson had a very private meeting."

Lyndon Johnson had decided not to run for re-election, but Bobby Kennedy had his own plans, wanting to be the next president, and believed that L.B.J. would be in his way. Johnson was a lot cagier than Kennedy gave him credit for, and instructed an aide to "bug" the meeting.

Clandestine recordings at the Oval Office were not uncommon. Every president back to Franklin D. Roosevelt made secret recordings. It was only Richard Nixon who got caught, and he paid the ultimate price of resignation and disgrace. There is little doubt that Bobby learned quite a lot from his brother Jack about taped meetings in the White House. Unlike the famous Nixon tapes, the Johnson-Kennedy recordings would never become public because Bobby Kennedy "exterminated" Lyndon Johnson's "bug."

Jack Anderson reported that Bobby Kennedy carried with him a very special briefcase. The Senator, who was Attorney General of the United States when Marilyn Monroe was found dead, and brother of the President, would never be searched by the Secret Service when entering the White House. Bobby Kennedy's briefcase carried more than papers and other things. Inside was a highly sophisticated anti-bugging jamming device. Over the years I have seen several. They cost many thousands of dollars. But Bobby Kennedy had his "security system" and he knew it was worth every cent that he had invested.

This device is capable of knocking out or jamming any transmission equipment. During that particular period of time there was also equipment capable of erasing tape recordings by creating a magnetic field that would leave a tape blank. I think that this would have been included in Kennedy's "James Bond" briefcase.

It is apparent that Kennedy was far more cautious when entering the President's home at 1600 Pennsylvania Avenue than when he was visiting Marilyn Monroe at 12305 Fifth Helena Drive in Brentwood, California. For if Bobby Kennedy had his "007" kit with him, the Monroe-Kennedy tapes would also have been exterminated. But getting back to the conversation between Bobby Kennedy and Lyndon Johnson: It must have been a heated one, for this much is revealed in history. Johnson, for some strange reason, chose not to run for re-election. Instead, the Democratic race became a struggle between Bobby Kennedy and Senator Eugene McCarthy. Johnson later publicly announced that he had decided not to run for re-election because of his health. There is quite a bit of speculation that his decision was greatly influenced by Bobby Kennedy, a person that he had never been fond of during any part of his life or his administration.

It was a well-known fact that Bobby Kennedy was a ruthless man, power-hungry, very determined to make an indelible imprint of his name on American history. And there is no doubt that this might have happened, but on the late evening of June 5, 1968, a 24-year-old Jordanian Arab would erase all of Bobby Kennedy's hopes. Sirhan Beshara Sirhan shot Senator Robert Kennedy in the kitchen of the Ambassador Hotel in Los Angeles after Kennedy had won the Democratic primaries in Oregon and California. The television cameras following Kennedy out the back of the hotel to avoid the crowd captured the incident on film, much as they did the shooting of his brother's assassin by the late Jack Ruby.

I never will forget that tragic night. It was only a few miles away from the hotel where Kennedy was shot that his opponent Senator Eugene McCarthy was sharing the television primary coverage as the votes were being tallied. My own presence was off-camera, because I was McCarthy's sole bodyguard.

It seemed that the McCarthy people wanted to maintain a very low security profile. I actually protested, advising them that as one man I could not provide adequate security among a crowd of thousands at the campaign headquarters. I was overruled by their decision, and they were paying the bill. The moment the news of Bobby Kennedy's assassination reached us, there was almost a panic. Senator McCarthy had very good reason to be worried. Perhaps there was a conspiracy to kill both candidates.

As a candidate, McCarthy also had a few secret service agents assigned to him. They were never identified to me, and I was supposedly his only bodyguard. For this assignment, I was heavily armed, in preparation, in the background. In addition to my revolver, I had a riot helmet and a riot shotgun, but I knew even a one-man army could not hold off a well-planned assassination. Within minutes, the McCarthy camp agreed to allow the Los Angeles Police Department to assist. That was a very smart move—a move that Bobby Kennedy earlier refused to accept.

As time goes by, the deaths of Bobby Kennedy and his brother before him will continue to be questioned by the public. So will that of Marilyn Monroe, for they all seemed to share a common bond. Many columnists, including the late Dorothy Kilgallen, had a theory that all three deaths were connected with each other. There is a certain amount of evidence that can be weighed on either side, I am certain. But the interesting thing is that they were all close friends, and Marilyn was linked romantically and had affairs with both of these top politicians. And all three were assassinated.

XV

Did Hoffa Blackmail the Kennedys?

It has been said that Bobby Kennedy was responsible for Jimmy Hoffa becoming the "Boss of the Teamsters." Then Bobby would lose quite a bit of sleep because he was doing everything in his power to put Hoffa in jail—or did he?

In 1955, Bobby Kennedy was a chief counsel for Senator John McClellan's Permanent Subcommittee on Investigations. The first important move that the committee decided to take was to implicate the (then) Teamster's president, Dave Beck, who was being accused of embezzlement of union pension funds. It was reported that Hoffa arranged for one of Beck's attorneys to turn over the evidence to Kennedy and the committee.

Therefore, Jimmy Hoffa became president of the union, and Kennedy thought Hoffa was just as corrupt as Beck and decided to use whatever powers he had to put Hoffa behind bars. Bobby was known to be very ambitious early in his political career. And as the years progressed, he was using that power wherever he could. He was obsessed with "getting Hoff." In 1961, he privately told Marilyn Monroe, "I will get this S.O.B., Hoffa, and put him behind bars."

Although the committee lacked certain jurisdictions over labor affairs, Bobby Kennedy did have the power to get Hoffa and to have the Senate Select Committee on Improper Activities in the Labor Management Field to be created. It was chaired by Senator McClellan, and Bobby served as chief counsel from its inception in 1957 through 1960. At that time, his brother John Kennedy was still a senator from Massachusetts, and he was also a member of the committee. This committee had an unofficial name—it was known in Washington circles as the "Get Hoffa Squad."

But Hoffa, like a sly old fox, never fell into any of Bobby Kennedy's traps. The McClellan Committee worked vigorously to indict Hoffa, but all of their efforts failed. But in 1961, Bobby's brother, then President of the United States, gave him "absolute power," naming him the Attorney General of the United States. This was the highest legal title and power in the United States, and a post that Bobby would hold until 1964.

As reported, Bobby Kennedy was seeing a lot of Marilyn Monroe during those summer months of 1962, after her relationship with Jack Kennedy broke off because of protests from his Jackie, who threatened to "walk out" on the President of the United States. This was something that the Kennedy family could not afford, especially since Jackie had threatened and almost done this a few years before. It is a well-known fact the Old Joe Kennedy, the father of the Kennedy boys, reportedly paid her off a large sum of money, estimated to be a million dollars cash.

It was also said, among those close to the Kennedys, that J.F.K. had sent Bobby to the West Coast to meet Marilyn and "put out the fire," meaning to make her quit calling J.F.K. at the White House. After all, Jackie had her own network of "spies" in Washington. It was also reported that when Bobby could not resist Marilyn's charms, J.F.K. became furious with his younger brother.

It was obvious that wiretapping and bugging were in use at any place Bobby Kennedy was known to frequent. And we must not forget that he frequented both Marilyn Monroe's Brentwood home plus the beach home of his brother-in-law, Peter Lawford, quite frequently on his numerous visits that summer of 1962 to Los Angeles. Jimmy Hoffa was the one who ordered the clandestine recordings. We must also take into consideration that, likewise, Bobby Kennedy was "bugging" Jimmy Hoffa.

This brings us up to the night Marilyn died. Her killers' voices were preserved forever on the bugged tapes, according to a very reliable source. Yet, while both J.F.K. and Robert Kennedy were alive, they never denied the rumors that they had been Marilyn's lovers, or that they had spoken to her by telephone, or were intimate with her in her own home and other places on several occasions.

The question is, what interest would Jimmy Hoffa have in Marilyn Monroe if she was not close to the Kennedy's? If Hoffa had the Spindel tapes, as reported, then why was it that he did not "go public" with them? At first I could not come up with an answer. But after a great deal of research, thought, and putting the pieces together, I think I discovered the solution.

Being a detective, I placed myself in Hoffa's shoes. What would I do if I were in his place? Tell the world about the Kennedys and Marilyn Monroe, give the media the tapes? Not at all. This would only infuriate the Kennedys, and they would come down on me like a ton of bricks. So the smart way to play it would be to make a deal. Some may call it blackmail, but in politics it's called "let's make a deal." If you lay off me, I will not...

Although we will never know if such a deal was actually

made, we do know that it was discussed, and logically this would be the best approach for all concerned parties. Yet, as driven as Bobby Kennedy was to put Hoffa away, even after he received absolute power as Attorney General of the United States, the union boss remained untouched. In 1965, Bobby Kennedy resigned as Attorney General and became a United States Senator from New York. His quest to nail Hoffa ended after a decade of effort.

Ironically enough, Hoffa was later sent to prison, not by Bobby, but by his successor, Nicholas Katzenbach, the new Attorney General of the United States, under the Lyndon B. Johnson administration. Then in 1975, after Jimmy Hoffa was out of prison, trying to regain his old position as head of the Teamsters, he would disappear, and his body never could be found. Shortly before he met his fatal destiny, Hoffa bragged that he had information that might critically embarrass the Kennedys. He referred to it as "seamy." Was he talking about the Marilyn Monroe tapes that had been recorded from her house, and those incriminating words on the tapes that reveal the identity of her killers?

This was just one of the many incidents, or coincidences, that took place in the wake of Marilyn Monroe's death.

Many of us knew Marilyn was killed because she knew too many government secrets, which she meticulously detailed in her red diary. Years later, her knowledge of these secrets would be made public.

XVI

The Senate Intelligence
Committee—1975

Exactly thirteen years after Marilyn's death, Senator Frank Church in 1975 formed and headed what was labeled the Senate Intelligence Committee. The purpose of this committee was to investigate the alleged subversive actions of the Central Intelligence Agency. This investigation was past due, as it has been reported that President Richard Nixon was on the verge of investigating the same activities conducted by the C.I.A. just prior to the time when he became deeply involved with Watergate.

There was much information that Frank Church and his committee pulled out of the C.I.A. files. Naturally, as in all investigations, particularly those in Washington, D.C., Church discovered that he had to wade through a lot of material before he got down to what he was really looking for. One of the first important points that the committee heard testimony on, and received evidence of, was that the C.I.A. had been very heavily involved in an effort to assassinate Fidel Castro in Cuba. After this was unveiled, the names of Bobby and John Kennedy surfaced in connection with this action, which had been instigated in the early months of the Kennedy administration.

Although the committee tried its best to keep the names of President John F. Kennedy and his brother Bobby out of the reports, they found it to be not just difficult, but impossible. The news leaked out, the press picked it up, and evidence emerged that was considerably embarrassing not only to the two deceased Kennedy brothers but also to Senator Ted Kennedy and the family in general. It also became a well-known fact that while John F. Kennedy was under sedation with his ailing back problem, Bobby Kennedy "ran the country on the day of the Bay of the Pigs," as he had confided to Marilyn back in the summer of 1962.

There was still another interesting discovery made, and that was the link between the underworld and the Kennedy administration.

As the committee continued its probe, mainly into the "Kennedy-underworld connection," one of President Kennedy's several girlfriends' name was mentioned— Judith Exner. This alone nearly caused a volcanic explosion that opened up the rest of the C.I.A. files to the public.

Miss Exner's identity was flushed out by the Senate Intelligence Committee, and the main thing that the Church Committee wanted to inquire about was if President Kennedy could have learned about the plot to assassinate Castro from Judith Exner. But here's where the chain of events took a sudden turn for the worse.

It was learned that Judith Exner had dated President John F. Kennedy not just a few times but "several" times, including spending a few weekends at the White House when First Lady Jackie Kennedy was elsewhere and sharing the same bed with President John F. Kennedy. Fortunately, Miss Exner was alive and living in San Diego, and when her name appeared in print throughout the world she decided to hold a press conference and make a formal statement concerning her involvement with President John F. Kennedy.

Miss Exner was quite open about not only her relationship with John F. Kennedy but also that she was dating at the same time Sam "Momo" Giacana, who was the Mafia boss of Chicago. It was revealed simultaneously that another one of her very close mobster friends was Johnny Roselli, who was quite pleased with his indirect connection with the White House.

Before Sam Giacana could be questioned by the committee, he was found murdered in his Oak Hill, Illinois, home. This was believed to have been ordered by his underworld superiors. Coincidentally, just a few months later, before he was able to be questioned, Johnny Roselli also was found murdered, floating in a barrel in Biscayne Bay, off the coast of Miami, Florida.

After these events had taken place, the Church Committee did not proceed too far beyond this point. It has been assumed by many political writers that Frank Church was apprehensive about some of the events he discovered and the facts his committee uncovered, which were embarrassing not only to a lot of people, but to the United States government as well—particularly the C.I.A., which was the target of his investigation.

It might be of historical interest here that the Central Intelligence Agency was originally conceived and created by the late President Harry S. Truman, and its sole purpose was to conduct covert actions outside the United States. For some reason, known only to those men who have suceeded Truman in the Oval Office and the various C.I.A. directors who have been appointed throughout the years, the C.I.A., even as far back as the Eisenhower administration, took a complete 180-degree turn and started conducting covert activities inside the United States. They were not supposed to do so, but they did, and this was continuing up to and through the administration of John F. Kennedy. In fact, President Kennedy and his brother Bobby used the C.I.A. for many undisclosed actions, which the Church Committee brought to light.

After a great deal of this information leaked out to the newspapers, Chairman Frank Church claimed that there was no evidence to prove that Judith Exner was a connection between the Kennedy administration and the underworld. He even said that the committee was only trying to avoid needlessly blackening the reputation of the Kennedys. This was adding fuel to the fire, for William Safire, a *New York Times* columnist, accused Church of a "cover-up" of the committee's findings. Church, speaking on behalf of his committee, denied the charge.

This sparked Judith Exner to hold her press conference, in which she admitted meeting President John F. Kennedy in 1960 in Las Vegas at a party thrown by Frank Sinatra. According to what she told the press, Sinatra had later introduced her to Sam Giancana, who in turn had introduced her to Johnny Roselli. She dropped a further bombshell, stating that she had visited President John F. Kennedy nearly two dozen times at the White House.

When the official White House logs of 1961 and 1962 were examined, they showed that Judith Exner had telephoned President Kennedy more than seventy times from her home in Los Angeles.

At this point, we must bring forth a set of very important facts which Marilyn noted in 1962 in her diary.

These are the things Bobby Kennedy told her, and the red diary in which she wrote down those conversations is the one she showed to my client.

The findings of the Church Committee proved the following information, which Marilyn had written down in her red diary:

1. There was a definite connection between the underworld and the office of the Attorney General of the United States, headed by Robert Kennedy, and it was established by the Church Committee that Bobby Kennedy had certain members of the underworld on the government payroll.

2. There was a plot by the Kennedy brothers to have certain members of the underworld, obviously under the command of Sam Giancana and Johnny Roselli, construct various plans and allegedly work these plans out with the C.I.A., to assasinate Fidel Castro in Cuba.

3. There is a brief mention of the assassination of President Raphael Trujillo of the Dominican Republic, which took place on May 30, 1961, Bobby Kennedy had also told Marilyn about this.

When Lyndon B. Johnson succeeded John F. Kennedy as president in November 1963, he discovered many things that the Kennedy administration had been involved with but had kept secret. In the last few years of his life, he publicly stated that he was appalled to learn that the United States had been "running Murder, Inc." in the Caribbean area.

The fact that Judith Campbell Exner became the first self-admitted girlfriend of President John F. Kennedy, as a result of her name being found in the C.I.A. files by the Church Committee, certainly cast a giant shadow over the Kennedy administration and its operations. The bottom line is that the entries Marilyn had made in her little red diary back during the summer of 1962 of what had been told to her by Bobby Kennedy had been confirmed thirteen years later by a government committee. It is the belief of many that keeping this diary—which Bobby Kennedy only learned about ten days before Marilyn's death—was enough reason to have her put out of the way. Sometimes keeping a diary is bad business, not too advisable when you're writing down information told to you by the Attorney General of the United States. I have always felt that Marilyn, in all her naivete and ignorance of political affairs, should be considered as having far more intelligence, for I am absolutely convinced that she knew she was holding the "trump card" against Bobby Kennedy.

There is no evidence that the diary exists today, although the stories of its existence in many states and countries throughout the world have been numerous. The only things that we really know about the diary are that it was last seen in the coroner's office, and that it disappeared less than forty-eight hours later, along with certain other personal items of Marilyn Monroe's. This just goes to prove that there appeared to be corruption in the coroner's office back at that time.

Of further interest were some of the news items that surfaced after the Senate Intelligence Committee had recessed. One of them was a statement from Truman Capote, a very close friend of the Kennedys, especially Jackie Kennedy, who confirmed to reporters that it was Bobby—and not J.F.K.—who was seeing Marilyn in those last few weeks of her life. Walter Winchell mentioned a certain Washington VIP who "failed" Marilyn on the night when she needed him the most.

Anyone who refuses to believe that Bobby Kennedy was having extramarital affairs should read a book entitled, *Those Wild, Wild Kennedy Boys*, published in 1976 by Pinnacle Books, written by investigative reporters Peter Brennan and Stephen Dunleavy. In their extremely well-written and well-researched book, they state that their investigation had proved that Marilyn Monroe had had an affair with J.F.K. when he was a senator, and even during the time he was President of the United States, before she was passed off to his brother Bobby. They also made another interesting statement based on their investigation. Five years after Marilyn's death, in 1968, Bobby Kennedy was again in Hollywood, having a clandestine affair with a very attractive brunette. According to published reports, this love affair was going on at the time of Bobby's murder at the Ambassador Hotel in Los Angeles. Brennan and Dunleavy actually interviewed the girl, whose identity they concealed for her safety, and wrote, '...he definitely was having a thing with Marilyn Monroe before she died,' the girl said. 'He told me that.'

A couple of years after the Senate Intelligence Committee investigation, we learned that President Richard Nixon had listened to some of the bugs from the Kennedy administration, and found them quite interesting. In the book, *The Final Days,* by Bernstein and Woodward, published in 1976, President Nixon stated that he didn't understand what Marilyn Monroe had to do with national security.

It is ironic that thirteen years after her murder, Marilyn Monroe's name surfaced in this committee's investigations along with those several other girls, including movie actresses, secretaries, and others too numerous to mention. Although Marilyn, in her time, perhaps did not realize she had so much competition, she certainly was the reigning queen of Camelot on the West Coast. One reporter even referred to her as "the First Lady of the West Coast," back when her love affair was going on with President John F. Kennedy.

In Arthur J. Schlesinger's biography, *Robert Kennedy and His Times*, which was a best-seller a few years ago, he wrote about the late Adlai Stevenson's observations of

Bobby Kennedy when he first met Marilyn Monroe in the last week of May, 1962, after she had sung "Happy Birthday" to President John F. Kennedy. The observation is quite interesting:

> We both met her [Marilyn] the same night after she had sung "Happy Birthday, Mr. President" at a Madison Square Garden celebration of John Kennedy's 45th birthday. It was May 19, 1962, at a small party given by that loyal Democrat Arthur Krim of United Artists. Adlai Stevenson wrote a friend about his "perilous encounters" that evening with Marilyn, "dressed in what she calls *skin and beads.*" I didn't see the beads! My encounters, however, were only after breaking through the strong defenses established by Robert Kennedy, who was dodging around her like a moth around the flame."

In this very same biography, to verify the fact that Marilyn Monroe had been calling Bobby Kennedy in Washington, the following account is quite important:

> There was something at once magical and desperate about her. Robert Kennedy, with his curiosity, his sympathy, his absolute directness of response to distress, in some way got through the glittering mist as few did. He met her again at Patricia Lawford's house in Los Angeles. She called him thereafter in Washington, using an assumed name. She was very often distraught. Angie Novello talked to her more often than the Attorney General did. One feels that Robert Kennedy came to inhabit the fantasies of her last summer. She dreamily told her friend W.J. Weatherby of the *Manchester Guardian* that she might get married again; someone in politics, in Washington...

Now through my investigation and the facts brought out

by the Senate Intelligence Committee, headed by Senator Frank Church, we have proven the following:

(a) Marilyn Monroe definitely did have secret and classified government information which was told to her by Bobby Kennedy.

(b) She had been involved both with John F. and Bobby Kennedy.

Through Arthur Schlesinger's excellent biography of Robert Kennedy, the following has been definitely established by the author, who was a close friend and confidante of both Robert and John F. Kennedy:

(a) Verification that from their first meeting, on May 19, 1962, in New York City, Bobby Kennedy was completely ecstatic over Marilyn Monroe.

(b) Verification that Bobby Kennedy was seeing Marilyn Monroe during the summer of 1962.

(c) Angie Novello actually had verified that Marilyn Monroe had talked not only to her but also quite often with Robert Kennedy, who was then Attorney General of the United States. There is verification by W.J. Weatherby of the *Manchester Guardian* that Marilyn had planned to get married again, to "someone in politics."

As I studied the results of the Frank Church committee, coupled with the biography written by Arthur Schlesinger, I realized that what Marilyn Monroe had told my client back in those days preceding her death in 1962 was absolutely true.

Some things about Marilyn Monroe's death were filed away, and never made public.

XVII

The Mystery of Jack Quinn

Just about a month before I took over the investigation of the Marilyn Monroe case, my client received a telephone call at his Columbia Pictures office, exactly at 11:30 a.m., Friday, August 4, 1972. Jack Quinn had called Slatzer from a pay phone because he could not call from work, as his job was in the microfilm department of the Los Angeles Hall of Records. His call had been prompted by a story of about a half page in which Slatzer was quoted as saying Marilyn Monroe did not commit suicide but had been murdered. It was a feature story in the Los Angeles *Herald Examiner* written by Wanda Sue Parrott.

Quinn had opened the conversation by telling Slatzer that he had received a call from somebody on the Board of Supervisors, questioning him as to whether anyone had called his department, asking for a particular microfilm concerning Marilyn's death that had been secreted away years ago.

Slatzer taped the conversation. Because of some telephone threats he was receiving at the time, he had decided to tape all strange phone calls. This call was taped in its entirety. For the benefit of the reader, we will not print the complete conversation, but include only the sections pertinent to the case. "Q" is Quinn; "S" is Slatzer:

Q. About that Parrott column today?

S. Yes.

Q. Well, let me tell you what happened then... Do you remember when the city went over to computer... Well, let me tell you something: You're right about the coroner's investigation. You're right about the injections, you know... Because, there were 723 pages in the original report, and they boiled that thing down to fifty-four pages...you know...the investigational report...but the investigation report at that time was the ten preceding days...they investigated back that far...they got ahold of people that had seen her, and so forth, and so on... Did you see photographs of her? ...the coroner's photographs of her that were taken in the bedroom?

. Down here, all the packages from the intelligence units from the sheriff's and police intelligence units, we micro [microfilmed] them *edited out of the final report.*

S. Why was that?

Q. Well, anyway, at the time...well, look, I just pulled the micro out to look at it again, 'cause when they changed the Hall of Records around down here, all the packages from the intelligence units from the sheriff's and police intelligence units, we micro [microfilmed] them things... We destroyed the original records, but a lot of them went onto microfilm. Now these were one of the ones that went on microfilm. A lot of the city and county stuff, you know, remains in packages...are stored in warehouses and stuff.

S. Right.

Q. But anyway, what happened was that at the time there were bruises. Now the injection was in the arterial artery under the arm... Yeah, a very small pin prick under the arm. She had a lot of bruises on her. She had seen Kennedy, you know, a couple of days before that.

S. Which Kennedy?

Q. Bob.

S. Bobby?

Q. Yeah. Bobby lied like a bastard, and not only that, and so did, you know, the actor...they lied like bastards. Now, Bobby went out to the house to see her, according to the police report. Now none of this ever came out at the time of the death, you know, there was all that bull about the President, and stuff...

S. Yeah.

Q. Now he [Bobby] was seeing her on a Saturday. It was in the report, you know. And he was coming out here, but anyway what happened was, according to the report, if I remember correctly what I looked through this morning, and I'm taking it out of context, you know. What happened was that she [Marilyn] was bugging John F., you know. [Editor's note: This is not to be confused with any telephone or house bugging.]

Quinn went on to say that Bobby Kennedy went to Marilyn's house, that there was an argument, that she got hysterical, and that a physician was with him. And that's where the injections came from. According to Quinn, they "hit" her, with phenobarbital and something else...

Quinn reiterated the fact that this 723-page report had been boiled down to fifty-four pages as the so-called autopsy report, but the whole 723 pages of the police report was put on microfilm. He claimed it was in the files at the Hall of Records.

Quinn went on to report that there actually had been a spinal tap made, which apparently was never listed, although it should have been made, according to most forensic pathologists. Quinn insisted that they had run a spinal tap which would have shed more light on how she died, and that the brain was never officially tested, only weighed. Quinn went on to talk about the involvement of the Kennedys and the mishandling of Marilyn's death investigation. He added the following:

> S. But everything in on microfilm, which is the original...
>
> Q. Well, you could petition the city for a hundred years, and they're going to just deny that it exists. But what they would release is probably the fifty-four some pages that they had taken at the time.
>
> S. But they didn't even release that.
>
> Q. They didn't release that?
>
> S. No, you mean the coroner's office?
>
> Q. Yeah, I mean not only the package with the investigation procedures, you know, from the police department and everything, and from the sheriff's department. The sheriff's lab wasn't too hot at that time, so the sheriff brought in the L.A.P.D. on it... In the house there, and everything... The pictures that were taken. They didn't disclose any bruises. The pictures were shot at angles where no bruises showed, like the bruises near the ear, you know.

Quinn insisted that there was a massive cover-up in both the L.A.P.D. and the coroner's office with regard to death of Marilyn Monroe. He further stated that this particular information had been placed on two reels of Olivetti microfilm. When this is copied, it is enlarged with a high-speed copier on special photographic emulsion stock that works only with this particular machine.

Slatzer agreed to meet Quinn in Hollywood at a certain delicatessen to have a quick bite of lunch and make arrangements with Quinn to copy the microfilm that afternoon. Their meeting was witnessed from an adjacent booth by Wilson S. Hong. Quinn said the paper would cost about $14.33 a ream and the whole thing would probably come to about $28 or $29. Although Slatzer offered to give him $35 cash, Quinn refused to take it.

The general converation with Quinn went as follows, according to notes that Slatzer made: The first portion of the tape goes into the area of responsibility. The second section deals with the investigation report of the L.A.P.D. The third section deals with the investigation report of the county sheriff. The fourth section contains memos and correspondence from all department heads back and forth to each other; that is, letters from the police commissioner to the coroner's office and law enforcement agencies on the Marilyn Monroe case.

"These pages," Quinn stated, "might incriminate John F. Kennedy, who was then the President of the United States. There were several memos found in her bedroom, slips of papers, phone numbers that she had been calling that day...all papers scattered around, quite a few, and all of them were microfilmed."

Part five contains statements, including a voluminous one from a high police official who was on an L.A.P.D. investigation team and actually went to Washington to get Attorney General Bobby Kennedy's statement.

Kennedy's statement was allegedly taken in 1962, right after Marilyn's death. Kennedy personally initialed the top and bottom of each page and signed under oath, Quinn said. The information it contained concerns Marilyn Monroe's involvement with his brother, John Kennedy, President of the United States. Robert Kennedy said that he had come to Los Angeles on the day of Marilyn's death, Saturday, August 4, 1962. According to the statement that Quinn read, Robert Kennedy had gone out to Marilyn's house to talk to her because there was the possibility of a divorce pending between First Lady Jackie and the President, J.F.K. Additionally, Quinn said Robert Kennedy stated that his brother J.F.K. was involved, that J.F.K. dispatched Bobby to come out to Los Angeles and talk to Marilyn because he was getting a lot of phone calls from her and was afraid of future embarrassment, and also that he was having plenty of marital problems at the time because of Marilyn's phone calls to the White House.

Bobby Kennedy also stated in the statement that he and an actor friend went to Marilyn's house the day of her death, late in the afternoon. There was a violent argument. Marilyn grabbed Kennedy. It was here, the high-ranking police official in Los Angeles had stated in his report, that Robert Kennedy was honest about the whole thing, that he was honest to the point that it embarrassed the L.A.P.D. here in L.A. Quinn stated that Bobby Kennedy said Marilyn had a few drinks and threatened to hold a news conference because she had been made certain promises by J.F.K., although he did not say what promises.

According to Quinn, Bobby had volunteered too much, perhaps so much that Marilyn Monroe's murder would never be connected with the Kennedy brothers, because this record would be guaranteed never to be opened under any circumstances.

According to Quinn, Bobby Kennedy was at Marilyn's house when she went into a tantrum. After reading the report, Quinn knew Marilyn was drinking, and he thought it might have been Scotch. (What she was drinking was actually important.) She had told Bobby she was tired of the whole thing—being a plaything, being called to a certain friend's house many times where they had prostitutes. She was tired of the whole damned mess. This is how Quinn politely described it.

As Quinn continued to unravel the facts in the 723-page file from memory, he stated that Bobby Kennedy had admitted that when Marilyn lunged at him in an argument he literally had to knock her down. She threatened him in her house on Fifth Helena Drive, and he had to knock her down a couple of times. The bruises, according to Quinn, were caused by that.

However, Quinn also said it was a matter of record that Dr. Ralph Greenson came to Marilyn's house at about 5:30 that evening, and that he admitted giving her a shot. He never told anybody what the injection consisted of, and he never stated in the official questioning *where* he gave her the shot. And then, according to Quinn at a later date in a follow-up police report, he contradicted himself.

Quinn also stated that according to the original report, Ralph Roberts, Marilyn's masseur, had called Marilyn because they were having a dinner date that evening. Dr. Greenson had answered the phone. Roberts knew Greenson's voice very well. Greenson had told Roberts, "She's not here."

Getting back to section six of the microfilm tape, Quinn states that this gets into the autopsy reports. This happens to be in two parts. Part one is pertinent information regarding the autopsy. Part two happens to be thirty-two photos of the body. The entire report is on two reels, one with the 500 exposures on it, the second with 240. Slatzer had asked why 240, instead of 223 to make a total of what Quinn had claimed was 723. Quinn replied that because the second reel also contained covers and title pages, there were seventeen extra pages.

Quinn had reluctantly taken Slatzer's $35 to pick up the paper on the way back to his office, so that he could run off as many copies of the Olivetti microfilm as possible. This would include the thirty-two pictures of Marilyn's body that had been taken by the authorities. The arrangement was to meet that night at 6:00 at the Smoke House restaurant in North Hollywood, near Warner Brothers Studios.

Slatzer and his friend Wilson Hong arrived at the Smoke House a little after 5:00 p.m., that same afternoon, and waited. Slatzer sat at the bar, where Quinn had agreed to meet him, while Hong as a witness, as he had been previously that day, sat several seats away. Six o'clock came and went. Quinn did not show up.

On Monday morning, Slatzer went down to the second floor of the Hall of Records building to locate Quinn. The mysterious tipster was described by Slatzer as a man in his early forties with slightly gray sideburns, a thick crop of curly dark hair, and a tanned skin that looked natural. When my client last saw Quinn, he was wearing brown horn-rimmed glasses, a short-sleeved shirt and matching pants along with an indentification badge like those worn by all employees of the county. It not only had his name on it, but also his picture.

The search for Jack Quinn that Monday lasted from the time the Hall of Records opened until it closed. Nobody had ever heard of the name Jack Quinn, and furthermore the personnel department did not have a Quinn listed as working in that building.

It was very strange. If Jack Quinn did not really exist, who was this person who was claiming to be Jack Quinn, and who knew so much about the case that has unfolded since but which was not known at that time? Could it be that certain records concerning Jack Quinn had been conveniently misplaced or destroyed, such as those in the case of Marilyn Monroe? If Jack Quinn was an imposter, what would he have to gain by contacting my client and reciting all this information, which was quite critical of the police department, the coroner's office, and the Kennedys?

Jack Quinn, today, remains a mystery man. But there was one thing about him that was not a mystery: He had his facts right. He knew certain things that were not to come to light until later on, and he verified certain things that had never been published before, which had been only known to my client and me.

Jack Quinn was for real, in my opinion. And somehow, somewhere, I have the feeling that he may surface, providing that he has not already been deep-sixed into the ocean.

XVIII

The Absence of Fingerprints

When Sergeant Jack Clemmons first arrived at 12305 Fifth Helena Drive the morning of August 5, 1962, he did not know how Marilyn Monroe had really died. He did not know whether it was suicide as reported, natural causes, or accidental. Of all the possibilities, the one which at the time he would suspect least would be murder. Until an official autopsy is performed, however, all of these causes should be suspected.

However, it didn't take the veteran police officer too long to reach one preliminary opinion: She just might have been murdered. He suspected foul play almost from the very beginning.

If Marilyn had died by the hands of another, surely the fingerprints of the guilty would be left in her bedroom where her naked body was found stretched face-down, swanlike, diagonally across her double bed. Twenty years later in Los Angeles, the police department's Scientific

Investigation Division Unit rarely takes fingerprints at the scene of a typical crime. With their limited staff, it would be virtually impossible to check for latent fingerprints on every crime, especially with the near-epidemic crime wave that has been going on in every major city. But there are exceptions. Even now, L.A.P.D. takes fingerprints in every case where homicide is *suspected.*

Jack Clemmons told his superiors that he suspected that Marilyn Monroe might have been murdered. Even if she had not been a noted celebrity, this respectable veteran police officer's opinion should have sparked at least a cursory police investigation. Marilyn's housekeeper and companion, Mrs. Eunice Murray, even told Clemmons that she suspected the house would be sealed up. Normally, as Clemmons observed and later told reporters, it was quite unusual for a housekeeper to have this unusual foresight.

Normally, when a housekeeper's employer is found dead under such circumstances, there is much grieving, and not much worry about getting rid of the perishables in the refrigerator, doing odd tasks around the house, and carrying small baskets out to a car, as Murray did while Clemmons waited in the bedroom for his relief officers to arrive.

A few hours later the L.A.P.D. was at full staff, ready to face the peak crime hours. The scientific investigation team was on duty, and they discovered that the house was indeed sealed off. Marilyn's body had been dispatched to Westwood Memorial Cemetery. The fingerprints of Marilyn Monroe's killers were obviously still in her bedroom, or someplace in the house, to say the least.

This may come as a shock, but none of the rooms in Marilyn's house was ever dusted for fingerprints. There is a notation on one of the police reports which states that "no latent fingerprints were taken."

Instead, as is the custom, the fingerprints of Marilyn Monroe's dead body were taken and rolled on to a standard fingerprint card, later to be classified for the record as 150 27-100 17 M 26 U 0116. Her fingerprints could not lead to her killers' identity. They just proved that the dead body had once been the shell of Marilyn Monroe, so that nobody would dispute the fact that she was legally dead.

Although there was some speculation at the time that the house had been clinically dusted by members of a government agency, so that no latent fingerprints could be taken, this was never proven. The information came from a very reliable source, but nobody was ever to prove or disprove this theory. What could have been proved, and never was, was the fingerprint evidence of who was really in Marilyn's house, particularly the bedroom. The prints would not reveal, scientifically, when her visitors were there, but they would point to one man—a man suspected of being deeply involved with Marilyn, and even said to be in her house late that Saturday afternoon.

Although he had denied being intimate with her, or ever being inside her home on Helena Drive, the fingerprints could have declared him to be a liar, not to mention a prime suspect in her murder. We have proof that Marilyn received this particular visitor late that Saturday afternoon, just a few hours before she really died (as it was later proved, Marilyn had been legally dead since approximately 9:00 p.m. Saturday night). Her visitor was seen in the vicinity at approximately 5:00 p.m., walking down the short block on Fifth Helena Drive, with another man whose identity could not be established, but who was carrying what resembled a doctor's medical bag. The fact that they were walking from the main street running off Sunset Boulevard, which is Carmelina Drive, to Marilyn's house indicated that for some unknown reason, or possibly a very good reason, they did not want to create suspicion by driving to the end of the small cul-de-sac.

Since the only way to enter Marilyn's house was to go down to the end of the cul-de-sac, they were observed from a nearby house where on the second floor a group of ladies met weekly to play bridge. This particular house is much closer to Carmelina Drive than to the entrance of Marilyn's house. But from the upstairs card room, one could look out and see who was going down Fifth Helena Drive, and the gates and front entrance of Marilyn's house were highly visible.

One of the ladies, all of whom were fairly elderly at the time, had glanced out of the window and seen Robert Kennedy and another man whose identity they did not know enter Marilyn's home.

The lady exclaimed, "Look girls, there he is *again*." A few of the other members of the card party went to the window, looked out, saw Robert Kennedy, and later verified that Robert Kennedy was at Marilyn Monroe's residence that afternoon.

It was verified by the Los Angeles Police Department that Robert Kennedy, Attorney General of the United States, had arrived Friday afternoon at the St. Francis Hotel in San Francisco with his wife and a few of their children. His purpose in coming to the Coast, allegedly, was to appear on the Ernie Kovacs television show on Sunday, August 5, make a speech to the San Francisco Bar Association on Monday, August 6, and then take a swing through the Northwest and look over various reservoir areas in an assessment for the Department of Interior. It has also been established that after Robert Kennedy checked into the St. Francis Hotel he surfaced early the next morning at the Beverly Hills Hotel registered under a different name.

He was seen around the hotel that morning and part of the early afternoon, before he checked out and was driven to Peter Lawford's beach home on Pacific Coast Highway.

One must remember that at the time, actor Peter Lawford was married to Pat Kennedy Lawford, the sister of J.F.K. and Bobby Kennedy. The house Bobby Kennedy went to that afternoon had been the once-swank summer home of film mogul Louis B. Mayer. Although the Lawfords had lived there for some time, the place was badly in need of repair.

The question that one must ask at this particular point is quite simple: Could it be that Marilyn's entire house had really been cleansed, as can be done by various knowledgeable government people, of any fingerprints whatsoever including Marilyn's? This is a theory that we should not disregard too readily. We have established the fact, and it has been proved through eyewitnesses, that Bobby Kennedy did visit Marilyn Monroe's house that Saturday afternoon. We have to assume that what the neighbors had seen and told us was correct. They would have no reason to lie. They had seen Bobby Kennedy come to the house more than one time.

A highly respected investigative reporter, Tony Sciacca, contacted me in 1975 when he was researching material for his book entitled, *Who Killed Marilyn?* with the subtitle *And Did The Kennedys Know?* Tony spent a great deal of time checking information my client and I had furnished to him and had done a further evaluation of the investigation of her death. He had considerable information from what he termed a very reliable source. After Marilyn's death, "The CIA came into Marilyn's home and made it sterile, and everything in the house," he reported. He even went further to say that every cup and glass, and anything with Bobby Kennedy's fingerprints, was cleaned or destroyed. The question is, why wasn't her room checked for prints? Maybe there were no prints after all! If there weren't, why go through the motions?

This certainly verified the information that we had on this case years before. So perhaps there was a good reason why the house was sealed, and why no latent fingerprints were taken.

We know Dr. Hyman Engelberg's fingerprints were left in Marilyn's house.

XIX

Dr. Engelberg—On the Spot

My personal telephone line started buzzing and I heard the voice of Alicia Sandoval, host of "Open Line," a live television program she hosts every afternoon on KTTV Television, a Metromedia Station, in Los Angeles.

"My guest today is going to be Dr. Hyman Engelberg, who pronounced Marilyn Monroe dead," she said. "Would you like to question him on television?"

I immediately jumped at the opportunity to pin him down. "How tough can my question be? And how long will I have?" I asked.

Alicia told me I could ask anything, and stay on the air as long as I wanted, or as long as the session could keep going.

"I don't want him to walk off the program angry, so let's hold your call until he is on for at least five minutes," Alicia suggested. Then she told me that Dr. Engelberg was scheduled to discuss heart attacks, plugging a recent book that he had written on his experience in the cardiac field. The date was September 24, 1982, and Alicia had called me less than an hour before broadcast time. I was given a special hot-line number to call, and the producer was alerted to put me through. I remarked to some of my staff, "I hope I do not give the good doctor a heart attack." Perhaps my reason for saying this was the fact that Dr. Engelberg has never, according to my information, talked publicly about Marilyn Monroe's death.

This would be my third appearance on Alicia's television show. The first was several months earlier when I was an invited call-in guest discussing missing persons investigations. And just a few weeks ago, I was an in-studio guest. The subject then was the investigation of the death of Marilyn Monroe that took place about the time of the twentieth anniversary of her death. Alicia was not playing the devil's advocate, but she treated the matter very fairly. After the show she told me, "I believe what you said, and I believe Marilyn was murdered."

Dr. Engelberg had become a very controversial figure in my investigation into Marilyn's death. There have been many unanswered questions, and I felt that he might well clarify a great number of them. Quickly, I sat down and prepared a list of about six or seven questions I intended to ask. As a professional investigator, I know that in any form of interrogation you make the first question easy to answer just to get the subject talking. The real key questions would naturally follow.

Alicia suggested that I watch the show while talking to Dr. Engelberg. Since I had a television in my office, my secretary turned it on to Channel 11. The good doctor was introduced by Alicia, and he appeared to be calm, professional and knowledgeable. The first caller discussed heart attacks and the following two-way interview went well. I would be the next "caller."

Regular callers gave only their first names. I fully identified myself, and just in case he had forgotten, which

I never believed he would, I added, "I'm the investigator who worked on the Marilyn Monroe case over ten years." I gave him my easy question to answer, which was as follows:

"Doctor, I have a couple little things I would like cleared up and I thought possibly you could do that for me. Just a couple of days [on August 3, 1962] before Marilyn died, you gave her an injection according to the probate claim that you submitted [he sent a bill to her estate for payment], and I wonder if you could tell what the injection was for, and why it wasn't shown on the autopsy, because it would have left a bruise?" (The injection *would* have left a mark, yet it was not reported in Noguchi's autopsy report.)

Dr. Engelberg made no vocal response. The host remarked that he did not hear my question and asked me to repeat it. That was unusual, as I heard it clearly off the television monitor and my staff that was watching also heard it. Alicia Sandoval heard it and she was sitting right next to him, but it seemed that everyone watching clearly heard it but Dr. Engelberg. Was he buying time to determine how to respond?

I started to repeat my original question, although not word for word. "I have a couple of small questions I would like you to straighten out if you would," when Dr. Engelberg interrupted.

Looking at my television, I now saw what appeared to be a very nervous man. He said, "I'm not interested in talking about Marilyn Monroe on this program. I won't answer any questions about her at this time." He had been introduced, by the way, at the beginning of the program, as the doctor who had pronounced Marilyn Monroe dead. What did he have to hide after twenty years? Why was he avoiding my polite question?

However, I must have had an ally somewhere out there in television world. A very knowledgeable, charming female voice broke through the barrier somehow, telling the person screening the calls that she was going to ask a medical question, and she asked Dr. Engelberg a very pointed question that everybody could plainly hear. In condensed form, her question went something like this: The lady caller had wondered why he had covered up the Marilyn Monroe murder, and she wanted to know how much the Kennedys had paid Dr. Engelberg and the other doctor for keeping her murder quiet all these years?

The doctor again stated to the host Alicia, that he did not hear the question. It was fairly obvious to us watching the little screen that Alicia understood the question, but she allowed the caller to ask it again. When Dr. Engelberg heard the question again, his expression changed completely—and he obviously *did hear* the female caller's question this time. He sat there looking as if he didn't even know what to say. Finally, Alicia Sandoval, good hostess that she is, interrupted the silence and suggested that perhaps Dr. Engelberg did not want to talk about Marilyn Monroe, since he had previously explained that.

When the program went off the air, Alicia called me. "Milo, as soon as we went to a commercial break, I talked about Marilyn, and he was very, very nervous. He was even skittish, off-camera."

I had advised the investigating team of the Los Angeles County District Attorney's office to watch this program, and they too noticed the doctor's nervous reaction to these two pointed questions.

A couple of weeks later, I was interviewed by a writer from the *London Times* who, in conversation about the Monroe case, told me that he had called Dr. Engelberg.

I asked if he granted the reporter an interview and what Dr. Engelberg had to say about the Monroe case.

The reporter said that the doctor seemed to be rather pleasant on the telephone but stated that since the Marilyn Monroe case has been reopened, and there obviously will be a grand jury inquest, he could not put himself into a position of answering any questions about the late actress.

I feel that Dr. Engelberg could tell us a lot, and it is my fervent hope that he eventually casts a light on some of the mystery that has been shrouding this case for twenty years.

XX
She Cried Out for Help

As the heavy doors of the psychiatric institution slammed loudly, closing Marilyn Monroe in from the rest of the world, she became extremely frightened and heartsick. She certainly was not acting as the tears welled up in her eyes, ran down her cheeks, and mixed with the mascara to form purplish-looking smears that almost gave her the appearance of having black eyes. She had literally been "taken prisoner" against her own will.

"I've always had a slight superstition about insanity," Marilyn told Bob Slatzer in late 1961. "It is said to run in my family, but I sometimes wonder. The only thing I really wonder about are some of those people who keep saying that someday I'll go crazy."

It was quite common in Marilyn's family for both her maternal grandmother and her mother to be institutionalized through the years. Marilyn's mother, Gladys Monroe Mortensen, was placed in an institution when Marilyn was less than one year old. In those days,

MARILYN MONROE: MURDER COVER-UP

they called such places "insane asylums" rather than the more kindly "sanitarium" or "institution."

We might go one more step back and mention that Otis Elmer Monroe, who married Marilyn's maternal grandmother, Della Mae Hogan, and Della Mae herself had been committed through the years by the courts to mental institutions. Della Mae had been born on July 1, 1876, in Missouri, and she died at the age of 51, just nineteen days after being committed for the third time to Norwalk State Hospital, which is now Metropolitan State Hospital in Norwalk. Her death on August 23, 1927, was attributed to myocarditis combined with manic depressive psychosis as the major contributing factor.

Her daughter, Gladys Pearl Monroe, was born in 1899 in Mexico, and went through two marriages, the first to a man by the name of John N. Baker, and the second to Martin E. Mortensen, who became Marilyn's father. He deserted his wife about three months before Marilyn was born at Los Angeles County General Hospital.

The fact that the maternal side of Marilyn's family had mental problems does not mean that they would necessarily be passed down to her. However, that is a question to which we will never know the answer. One thing we do know for sure: Marilyn Monroe had no apparent mental problems during her thirty-six years on this earth.

But Marilyn Monroe *was* committed to the Payne-Whitney Psychiatric Clinic in New York City during the month of February 1961, a short time after her divorce from playwright Arthur Miller. Marilyn's New York psychiatrist, Dr. Marianne Kris, recommended that Marilyn check into the clinic for what Marilyn believed to be only a routine medical checkup. She was not aware at the time that it was a hospital for the mentally ill.

After she was led into a room with metal door and bars across the window, and the door slammed, Marilyn screamed. "What the fuck are you doing to me? I don't want to be in this crazy house! I'm not insane! I'm Marilyn Monroe!"

Marilyn panicked when she discovered that the door was locked from the outside. Even her toilet was locked, and to use it she had to call a nurse. She wondered what these people were doing to her, caging her in a strange place like an animal and staring at her through an observation window about one foot square in the heavy metal door.

Her room had only a bed, chair and dresser. Writing material was completely forbidden. However, in desperation, Marilyn acquired a pen and a single sheet of paper, and hastily wrote a heartbreaking letter to her acting coach, Paula Strasberg. It was addressed to Lee Strasberg, Paula's husband. Both had been very close to Marilyn, and they were also very close to Marilyn's psychiatrist, Dr. Marianne Kris.

It was quite a convenient relationship, for Marilyn was generating a lot of income at the time, and it seems apparent that the Strasbergs had virtually mesmerized Marilyn into doing anything that they wanted. They were the ones who introduced her to attorney Aaron Frosch, who went with Lee Strasberg and Frosch's secretary to Marilyn's apartment one winter morning in New York to have her draw up a will that she was not in the frame of mind to write.

She had told Strasberg when he called that she did not want to draw up a will at that time, in January of 1961. Conveniently, Strasberg and Dr. Marianne Kris were outstanding beneficiaries in Marilyn's will. The will, incidentally, was not contested, but there was a court hearing ordered on the validity of it, because of the circumstances I have described. This was originated by Marilyn's former business manager and close friend who decided to remain on the West Coast, Mrs. Inez Melson.

The court hearing turned out to be futile, and Mrs. Melson, after much time and expense in New York City, lost her case.

The Frosch incident was one reason why Marilyn had told my client that she wanted to change her will, which she had planned to do the afternoon of August 6, 1962.

Robert Crivell of Commack, New York, owns a very interesting letter. He is the President of the Marilyn Monroe Fan Club-East. "I fell in love with Marilyn in 1960 and never stopped," he told me. "I never believed she committed suicide."

Crivell said that when he purchased the letter, which Marilyn wrote to Strasberg from the Payne-Whitney Psychiatric Clinic in New York City, he had to agree not to make it public until Lee Strasberg was deceased. He kept his word, for Strasberg died in February 1982. That seemed to have been a strange request, but considering the fact that Marilyn Monroe had told Slatzer that the Strasbergs were responsible for putting her into that situation, it is no wonder Lee Strasberg did not want this to come out until after his death.

For the purposes of record and interest to the readers, the letter is as follows:

> Dr. Kris has put me into the hospital...under the care of two idiot doctors. They both should not be my doctors. You haven't heard from me because I'm locked up with all these poor nutty people. I'm sure to end up a nut if I stay in this nightmare. Please help me Lee, this is the last place I should be—maybe if you call Dr. Kris and assure her of my sensitivity and that I must get back to class so I'll be better prepared... [She continued the rest of the letter on the reverse side of the paper, which was not a custom that Marilyn Monroe had.]
>
> Lee, I try to remember what you said once in class "that art goes far beyond the science."... Please

help me, if Dr. Kris assures you that I am
alright—You can assure her I <u>do not</u> belong here!
[She signed her name and then she added a P.S.]
I'm on the dangerous floor. It's like a cell.

In analyzing this letter it might be interesting to
understand that the underscores are Marilyn's. The letter
is quite a logical letter, and it certainly does not sound like
a letter written by somebody who has psychiatric
problems. The letter seems to cry out for help, but it is not
like a lot of the jumbled letters that quite commonly come
out of such institutions. However, Lee Strasberg took no
heed of this letter, nor did Dr. Kris. When Marilyn was
taken out of the hospital, it was by her second husband,
Joe DiMaggio. DiMaggio walked in, took her out of the
place, and then placed her in Columbia Presbyterian
Hospital, where she recuperated.

The interest to us again was Marilyn Monroe's will. The
reader should be reminded that she did have an
appointment with her attorney Milton "Mickey" Rudin to
change her will. She told my client less than twenty-four
hours before she died that she was cleaning up her life and
"getting rid of the leeches" and putting things back in
order. In fact, on that same day she told Slatzer that she
had fired Paula Strasberg and had written her a check for
a one-way airline ticket to New York City. Perhaps there
were several underlying reasons for this change that
Marilyn was making in her life. I am sure there were other
changes that were to be included.

In the same phone call in which Marilyn told Slatzer
about getting her life in order and the firing of Paula
Strasberg, she also told him with a trace of bitterness in
her voice that the Strasbergs were "into me" for several
thousands of dollars. They had been playing the stock
market, Marilyn confided to Slatzer, and had been
draining her dry financially with their losses, which she
was covering. No wonder she decided to sever the

relationship.

Moreover, the Strasbergs were literally "set up" by having a name like Marilyn Monroe in their acting school. On her reputation, the salesmanship went out, and students from all over the nation flocked to attend the Strasberg school, thus making him a wealthy man and introducing him into a world of Hollywood he had not known before. Again, it proves that Marilyn had a tendency to associate herself with a lot of the "wrong people" and that this tendency was to lead to her eventual death.

XXI
The Kidnap Plot

Back in the early thirties, the world was in fury when the first-born son of Charles Lindbergh was kidnapped and murdered. The year was 1932. The place was New Jersey. Bruno Richard Hauptmann was finally convicted, despite protests of his innocence, of murdering and kidnapping Lindbergh's young son, and paid his penalty on the gallows. This ultimately brought about what was known as the "Little Lindbergh Law," calling for the death sentence for any kidnapping.

Thirty years later, on August 6, 1962, the world almost became outraged again over a plot to kidnap Marilyn Monroe. I say "almost outraged," because that's the way it would have been had this well-planned plot taken place. The Lindbergh and Monroe crimes would have gone down in history as two of the most notable kidnappings of this century.

Through a quirk of fate or circumstance, Marilyn Monroe inexplicably escaped her fate of being kidnapped. Ironically, she would be murdered the day before.

My client and I first learned of the kidnap plot around 1977. Unlike most kidnappings, the victim would not be held for ransom, and contrary to the fate of the Lindbergh infant, the kidnappers had no plans of murder.

After receiving what we deemed reliable information about the existence of the kidnap plot, Slatzer and I got together for another of our many strategy meetings. These had become quite common since I had agreed to take over the case.

This particular consultation would not be in either of our offices. Without notice, I telephoned Slatzer at his home and said, "I'll be by in an hour. Meet me out in front."

I just didn't want to take any chances. I'm not paranoid about being bugged, but almost every day agents from Nick Harris Detectives are retained to detect clandestine bugs and wiretaps. With something this sensitive, I was not going to take any chances.

Slatzer was waiting outside when I arrived. He got into the car and we took off through the Hollywood Hills.

"Did I catch you at a bad time, Bob?" I asked.

"No," he replied, "I was just going over some notes when you called, and from the way you sounded, I felt this might be more important."

It *was* important. The new information we discovered made it more difficult for us to put together the puzzles in their proper perspective. We now had a kidnap plot slated for August 6, and the actual murder the day before.

The plan was to kidnap Marilyn Monroe from her Brentwood home, sedate her, and then fly her to an undisclosed place on the outskirts of Alexandria, Virginia, where she would be kept under sedation for about one week. The reason for this was to keep her from dragging the White House into the public eye and simultaneously to destroy her diary, thus discrediting all the things she had said Bobby Kennedy had told her and which she had entered into her little red book.

We had discovered that this plan was to have been put

into effect, supposedly by sympathizers of the Kennedys, but obviously another faction was working at the same time to silence her. Now here we had two operations, each one operating independently of each other, each one with the Kennedys' interests at heart, but so separate from each other that neither knew what the other was doing.

The kidnap plot feasibly could have worked quite well. The reasoning behind it included Marilyn's mother and maternal grandmother having had mental problems and spending most of their lives in institutions. Marilyn, against her will, as I described in the foregoing chapter, had been purposely placed in the Payne-Whitney Psychiatric Clinic in New York.

The plotters, of course, would say that Marilyn lost her mind temporarily, had perhaps gone crazy, and would discredit just about anything that she might say. After all, there was a convenient record set up that she had been in the "nuthouse", i.e., the Payne-Whitney Clinic, before. This would hold water, and provide a background of Marilyn's having had psychiatric problems, even though she never had. And the business about her having the two psychiatrists, Dr. Kris and later Dr. Greenson, would also be convenient documentation.

However, the "death" team arrived at her Brentwood home *first* and gave her the fatal injection of barbiturates—enough to kill a healthy cow, according to two prominent forensic pathologists—and she lay dead before the kidnap team could get to her.

As I weighed the plot to kidnap Marilyn Monroe, it became more reasonable to believe that she would be alive today had the "kidnap team" arrived first. According to our source, however, her death saved them a lot of risky work. Now that she was dead, she was silenced forever.

The plot actually had been simple rather than complex. Marilyn had told a few persons, other than Slatzer, that last weekend of her life, that if she did not hear from

Bobby Kennedy, she was going to hold a news conference and blow the lid "off this whole damned thing."

When Slatzer asked her what she meant on the evening of August 3, 1962, she merely replied that on Monday, August 6, she was going to hold a news conference and tell the media about her affairs with John and Bobby Kennedy, reveal the contents of her diary, and announce her future plans which included resuming filming of the picture, *Something's Got To Give*.

"I can care less," she told Slatzer, in a carefree attitude.

"But what about your diary?" Slatzer asked over the long-distance wires.

"It's safe," Marilyn replied. "Now, since my file cabinet has been broken into twice, I keep it in one of my big purses all the time."

"You're carrying around a walking time-bomb," Slatzer advised her.

Marilyn only laughed. "It just might explode in the wrong faces."

From the tone of her voice, Slatzer told me that he felt this diary about her affairs with the Kennedy brothers was her ace in the hole. But although she might have considered it as her weapon to get back at the Kennedys, her plans were soon to backfire.

This kidnap plot, strange as it seems, was told to Slatzer by a man who was at the time involved in an investigative arm of the Justice Department.

Not all of our informants were "highly placed." Some were even quite bizzare.

XXII

Tales of Bizarre Tipsters

As a private detective, my investigation into Marilyn Monroe's death was not the ordinary run-of-the-mill case. In most assignments of this type that Nick Harris Detectives have worked on in the past, informants usually do not come to us. In fact, we look for them. But this was not the typical case. A great many tipsters surfaced who offered to provide pieces of the missing puzzle. A great many of them threw us off the trail. And a lot of them just disappeared or were never heard from again after the initial contact.

However, in my business, even the craziest phone call has to be checked out. There always exists that one possibility that can lead to another, which could ultimately lead to something. And although in this case most of these roads led to dead ends, some of them were quite interesting.

A considerable number of psychics volunteered their services. In looking back over the records, I find that more offers to solve this murder mystery came from psychics than any other individual profession. Although I'm not totally convinced of their powers, I do realize that many psychics are credited for solving crimes in cooperation with various law enforcement departments throughout the world.

I agreed to attend a seance with one of them. Within a few minutes, the medium claimed that she had made "voice contact" with Marilyn. I ended up talking with her "spirit." It was not an unusual conversation, but there were long pauses between the answers. Sometimes there was no answer at all.

I purposely made my preliminary questions rather basic, things anyone who followed Marilyn Monroe's career should know. Then I asked what I considered a loaded question: "Marilyn, a few months ago your Uncle Wayne called and asked how I was doing on the case. He said he was calling on your princess telephone. Did you give it to him?"

"Oh,"the spirit voice replied, "I miss Uncle Wayne so much. He used to like dialing my phone, pushing those small buttons, so I gave him mine and ordered another..."

I had nothing further to say to "Marilyn." I was no longer interested in talking to the so-called spirit voice. She never had an Uncle Wayne. And the princess pushbutton telelphones were not even in circulation back in 1962.

This was just one of the crazy things that I decided to check out.

One thing that I have discovered is the fact that even criminals squeal. A convicted felon in Folsom Prison, in Northern California, called and said "If you want to know who off-ed Marilyn Monroe, I'll tell."

This seemed as if it might be a pretty good lead, because the man's voice sounded sincere. However, the first thing I would have to do would be get a lawyer to try and arrange a temporary release. The felon made it very clear that I would have to act fast. He assured me that his very good friend, "The Sheik," would soon "spring him." I decided to let The Shiek give him his freedom.

Then from a pay phone somewhere in Florida, a woman stuttered, "I have been communicating with Marilyn for years. She sends a letter every week."

This tipster sounded a little bit too tipsy for me to tackle.

The red diary was to surface again. I made a public announcement at a news conference during the first week of August 1982 that Nick Harris Detectives would pay $10,000 for the diary. Within a month, reports of its location came from 37 states, plus the Phillipines, Canada, Germany, England, and Australia.

All of those leads proved worthless, but one that I thought might be genuine came in at 8:40 a.m., August 4, 1982. The voice said, "I know where her diary is, Mr. Speriglio. It's been a while since I had it. But I can get the book." These were the first words spoken to me by Ted Jordan, the actor who would later receive worldwide attention in his claim to having Marilyn's red diary.

He further went on to say that the diary was in a box that was stored in the garage at a friend's house. It was among a lot of other memorabilia of Marilyn's. Jordan didn't disclose any of the contents.

Later he would admit lying to me, to the district attorney, and to the world. But at that time I believed him. In fact, a lot of people did, and all of the major wire services and newspapers throughout the world carried the story. I was hoping that the man was telling the truth and was right because he came on rather strong, extremely confident, and he sold me a bill of goods. But then again, he was an actor.

I decided to run a fast background check on him. He was fifty-four years old, a semi-retired actor, who had once been under contract at Twentieth Century-Fox Film Corporation when Marilyn was a contract player there in the late '40s. He also had played a small role as a blacksmith in the last few years of the long-running

"Gunsmoke" television series. I also learned that he had once been married to the famous strip-tease artist, Lily St. Cyr. His late uncle was the famous band leader, Ted Lewis. He had been born in a small town in southern Ohio, and his uncle Ted Lewis had been born and had been buried in his home town of Circleville, a town that pops up once a year in the news for having the noted annual pumpkin festival. Also, Jordan's real name appeared to be Eddie Jordan Friedman.

Unlike the other tipsters, he never discussed the reward. However, my $10,000 reward was topped by one of $100,000 within forty-eight hours by John Bowen, an antique dealer in Beverly Hills, who represented someone he identified as a "wealthy industrialist." He would not identify his client, except as being a person who wanted the diary for a private collection, and I wondered about the reason for secrecy. Later I would meet this client and find him to be legitimate.

To my surprise, my contact with Ted Jordan continued even after the much larger award was offered, and then upped from $100,000 to $150,000. I then began to believe that somebody really wanted the diary, but bad. I also was to find out that Jordan was negotiating with Bowen. It's amusing that two persons were offering rewards and each knew that Jordan had contacted both, claiming to have the much sought-after diary of Marilyn Monroe.

It became a waiting game at this point. Finally, Jordan broke his silence and publicly disclosed that he had the "real" red diary. The very first news story broke on August 18, 1982, in a copyrighted story by Cindy Craft, a reporter with the *Citizen-Journal*, a Scripps-Howard newspaper in Columbus, Ohio, Jordan's home state. The story broke on the UPI wire service, and immediately the Associated Press and UPI called for my reaction. I explained to them that Jordan and I had been in communication but he failed to show me the missing diary.

On that particulary day, Jordan was probably one of the most sought-after individuals in the world. Virtually every reporter wanted to talk, interview him, and my office received a barrage of phone calls asking how to reach him. But Jordan was now conveniently unavailable. Some of the media even managed to get his unlisted home phone number, but all they would reach was a recorded message on his home answering machine.

Ted Jordan was nowhere to be found. He had virtually disappeared. In fact, in my somewhat suspicious mind, I was actually quite concerned as to whether he might have ended up as a victim of foul play. I tried to shove that thought out of my mind, but in my business one has to figure all angles.

One veteran reporter, Jack Schermahorn, the West Coast representative of the New York *Post*, received a tip revealing Jordan's location. Hot on Jordan's trail, Schermahorn had an unfortunate major automobile accident. He was not seriously injured, but he was greatly shaken up and his new car was completely totalled. As Schermahorn lay convalescing at home, he listened to the announcements on televison stating that the elusive Jordan could not be reached by the media and was becoming known as the "elusive actor."

It reached the point that even the office of the Los Angeles County District Attorney wanted to talk with Jordan. The only one who knew his whereabouts was the reporter from his home town newspaper. She swore to keep it a secret, and she did.

A news item said that Jordan was staying at his mother's house in San Diego. Reporters called every Jordan listed in the phone book to no avail. I decided to track him down. It took just about an hour. His mother, I discovered, was not named Jordan and was living in Laguna Beach, several miles north of San Diego. I obtained both her address and phone number and decided to call. After I properly identified myself, his mother said, "Ted's not in now. But I will tell him to call you, Milo."

During a later conversation, Jordan told me that his mother suggested he talk to me. He didn't return my call, but he did break his silence. Again, the Associated Press called for my reaction. The reporter's voice on the phone said, "Jordan said he never had the diary. He only has a book of poems, which he and Marilyn once shared."

There was a long pause. The reporter obviously was waiting for me to say something. I kept my silence. The reporter continued, "And he further claims that the book was stolen from his car last night."

My instant reaction was, "incredible–unbelievable." I just did not buy his story. In fact, I seriously questioned how Marilyn's red diary, like magic, had turned into a book of poetry. And even more bizarre, why would it be stolen from his car? Nothing added up. I smelled a rat right away. Now I wasn't going to believe anything that Jordan would add to this. What could he do for an encore?

A short time later Jordan called me. "Milo, there are things I cannot talk about. I had threatening calls. They even called my mother's house. Please trust me. I have much to say to you, but not now."

I told Ted Jordan I could not buy his story on the "poetry book" that was purloined from his car. He told me it was not true. He just did not want the press climbing all over him.

I really did not know what to believe now. Here we had two different stories. First he announced to the world that he had Marilyn's diary. Second, what he had turned out to be a book of love poems, which was stolen from his car. Then he told me this was not so. My patience was growing thin.

After these choice little incidents, the news media were no longer interested in what Ted Jordan had to say. In fact, I felt sorry for him, but I could not lend any credence or respect to any of his doings. Then he again called me at home one night and said, "I think I'm becoming paranoid. I want you to know you have been very trustworthy. I'm going back East on October fourteenth and hold a news conference. I want to clear my name. I'll tell you more before I go." That was the end of that conversation. I felt that Jordan would have a difficult time convincing the press of his credibility after pulling off the diary hoax.

I did not hear from him again until the morning of September 19, 1982. He said, "I just cannot get to sleep any more. This whole thing bothers me."

I was tired of playing games with him by this time and decided to pin him down once and for all. "Ted, I want you to level with me," I began. "I don't buy all your bullshit. Now I want the truth."

Jordan replied that he trusted me and would share his secret, known only to his mother and his brother. "I do have a diary that belonged to Marilyn," he confessed. "I'm afraid someone will kill me for it. For a while I even carried a gun. Yes, I lied to the district attorney's office, the press, everyone, and I am sorry I ever talked to anyone about it." For some reason, he seemed to be quite concerned now about his safety. And if he had the original diary written during the last few weeks of Marilyn's life, he might have had something to worry about.

"No bullshit, Ted," I said. "Do you have the diary I want?"

"Not exactly," he answered meekly. "What I have is a red book, and it says the word 'Diary' on the cover, and Marilyn Monroe wrote some cryptic notes in it."

"What year was the diary written?" I asked.

Jordan replied that there was no reference to any specific year, but from her writing he speculated that it took place during 1959 or 1960.

I pressed him further and asked him how he obtained the diary.

Without hesitation he answered, "She left it at my place one day in 1959 or 1960 when I lived at Phyllis Place."

I had no evidence that Ted and Marilyn were in contact with each other in 1959 or 1960.

"Were all the pages filled?" I asked Ted.

"No," he replied. "She skipped weeks at a time, and there's probably only about thirty-two or thirty-three pages written on."

This would only account for about ten percent of the year, and it is highly unlikely that a person who chooses to keep a diary would not make more entries. I have found that people who go to the expense of buying a diary are quite conventional in their methods of keeping track of what they do on a daily basis, which is why they buy the little books in the first place.

Two things I wanted to know were why he changed his mind and why he said the diary had been a book of poetry.

"They were just love poems. She wrote them down in the diary." Then he went on to explain that the poems were all what he called "downers," but this was what she liked. "I want to recite them all to you someday." But then he explained that the diary was not just a book of poems.

The media were later to say that Jordan was a publicity seeker. He failed to show up for a scheduled conference with John Bowen, who had a cashier's check made out for $100,000 in his name. The antique store purposely had closed that afternoon, posting security guards around the place, waiting for Jordan, who never showed. His failure to show is what resulted in Bowen raising his reward to $150,000.

The unidentified client who wanted to buy the red diary was finally revealed. His name was Douglas Villiers, from London, England, and he was the wealthy owner of Antiquarius Antique Market in Beverly Hills. This particular market is a two-story structure housing millions of dollar's worth of precious antiques.

When I discovered this, my earlier doubts about the

buyer were erased. I was invited to dine with Bowen and their publicity man, Chris Harris. They made it clear the diary was sought only for its nostalgic value. I had reason to believe these men. Even without the political implications that were contained in the diary I was after, Jordan's earlier diary would still be a collector's item. But I remembered that Chris Harris had earlier told a newspaper reporter that "Jordan probably holds the key to this whole mystery." He added, "If he doesn't, he's right up there with Melvin Dummar and Clifford Irving in the Howard Hughes hoax."

It must have been destined for Ted Jordan and me to meet face to face. At exactly 10:32 a.m., Tuesday, September 21, 1982, he arrived in my Van Nuys office and apologized for being two minutes late. He carried a large, brown briefcase.

"My real name is Eddie Jordan," he said nervously. "But you can call me Ted. Milo, I want you to understand I'm not a clown. I really knew Marilyn." He then boasted about numerous sex affairs he had had with her. This was not of any importance to me, and I was actually getting tired of hearing the reports of all the men who claimed that Marilyn Monroe had to pull them into bed. A lot of tripe, in my opinion. I knew that Marilyn had affairs with a lot of men, but that was the last thing I wanted to discuss with Jordan.

"I wanted to marry her," Jordan said almost tearfully.

Instead, he had married Lily St. Cyr, and he handed me a book she had published in France. He pointed out their wedding picture. "I was the only one of her husbands whose photograph is in her book," he said.

I began to wonder why Ted Jordan was trying to prove himself to me. Next he took out two scrapbooks. Both of them contained what appeared to be genuine studio photographs and newspaper clippings that established his acting career, the kind most actors accumulate over a period of years. He showed me several still photographs from movies in which he had had small parts.

He then showed me a scar on his right hand, the one he told the press was the result of a blood ceremony that he and Marilyn had shared by cutting themselves and pressing their wrists together, vowing to share their future wealths, much in the tradition of the early Indians.

It might be interesting to note here that a scar on Marilyn's wrist, had it been like the one that Jordan exhibited, would have been one of the first things that would have been recorded by the coroner's office, because scars are very seldom overlooked. Needless to say, Marilyn would never cause such a scar deliberately.

Since Jordan hails from the Buckeye State, Ohio, he began to show me some photographs taken near his home town, where one of the last of the Indian wars was fought high up in the hills. He said, "Marilyn and I once carved our names up there," pointing to the approximate location. It might be interesting to point out here that Marilyn had never been known to visit that particular part of the country.

It seemed that after all these weeks of suspense, I was about to learn the location of the "diary" Jordan had told the world he had. He held up a photograph of what resembled a small mountain top, which actually was a hill back in Ohio, and said, "Look here, Milo, this is where I buried her diary."

"You buried it?" I asked in total astonishment.

"After Marilyn's death, I got a small metal container, took a sterling silver bracelet she gave me, a dress she left behind, and the diary, wrapped it up good, dug a hole—the ground was hard—my father watched—and I buried it," Jordan told me.

Jordan's explanation left me speechless.

His final departing words were, "I buried them in her memory." I felt a little bit sorry for him after he left the office. Perhaps I should have felt offended, or angry, but it didn't seem worth it.

Once again Ted Jordan made the news. The October 15, 1982, issue of the (Los Angeles) *Daily News*, carried the following headlines:

Book buried on Ohio hilltop!
Actor to give Marilyn Monroe's
diary to DA, newspaper reports

Similar stories appeared worldwide. Many people were convinced the real red diary had been discovered, and the mystery ended. Jordan had announced his diary did not contain references to political figures, and charged that the diary I and others had talked about was "fabricated to sell books."

Jordan claimed the diary he had unearthed contained love poems and various names and addresses. It was marked 'Traveling Diary' on the cover. Earlier, he had told the press he had the diary we were seeking, and it did contain references to the Kennedys. As you will recall, he later changed his story, saying it was just a book of poetry, then claimed it was stolen from his car.

The diary Jordan has cannot be the mysterious diary stolen from the coroner's office. By Jordan's own admission, he "found" it in 1959 or 1960. Marilyn Monroe did not even know Bobby Kennedy until May 1962, and the real diary we are seeking primarily contains statements he made to her. Both UPI and AP wire services were advised of the conflicting dates, yet I have not seen this appear in any newspaper. One top reporter I know told me, "Jordan is not worth giving any more ink to. The story will soon die."

"I want Milo Speriglio right now," a very demanding voice told my secretary.

"You tell him that this is General _____, former head of the C.I.A.—and I want to talk about Marilyn Monroe."

My secretary scribbled a note, entered my office, and suggested that I take this call immediately. I picked up the phone and heard the gruff voice. "General," I said, "I understand you want to talk to me." I had talked to several generals before in my life, but this time I was a little bit bewildered. I could not imagine what the ex-chief of the C.I.A. wanted to tell me.

"I read about you in the papers," he said. Then he started telling me about the "company" (the Central Intelligence Agency) and the operation he headed. The general was very talkative. He was dropping all kinds of important names, events, and things that only the C.I.A. should know. Strangely enough, Marilyn's name was never mentioned.

"General, " I interrupted, "I understand you called to tell me something about Marilyn Monroe. I don't care about the events around the world or what the C.I.A. has done or is doing, I'm just interested in investigating her death, and if you've got something to tell me, I'd like to hear it."

"Marilyn was murdered," he replied. "I knew her well. They killed her, poor thing. They tried to kill me, too, tried to put poison in my food."

"Who killed Marilyn?" I asked.

"The C.I.A." he answered bluntly. "They killed her..." He started to name persons, most of whom I had never heard of. A few minutes later the general dropped the bomb when he said, "I don't like to talk abut this, but Howard Hughes was my father." I started to question that, and he began to rattle on about other C.I.A. covert activities. By the time he got through, his credibility was quite diminished, and far as I was concerned, but I let him finish.

Then he dropped another bomb that really exploded

226

when he said: "I want you to know, I'm a very important man." In the background, I heard a woman tell him to keep quiet. He continued, and said, "No one knows this, but I am the *real* father of Elvis Presley."

The conversation came to a fast end. "With all due respect, General," I said, " I do not want to take up any more of your busy time. However, thank you for calling me and good-bye,"

As I placed the phone back on its cradle, I leaned back in my chair, stretched my arms, and took a deep breath. I was ready for the seventh inning stretch.

A lot of individuals will read about a murder or some other crime in the news, and then all of a sudden admit to it. It is a well-known fact among law enforcement agencies that there are dozens upon dozens of confessions to the same crime by people who cannot even place themselves in that part of the country on the particular hour or date that a crime occurred. If my client and I were to combine our files on all the kooks that we have talked with, of all the wild goose chases that we have gone on, while trying to get a better handle on the Marilyn Monroe case, it would fill several books this size.

XXIII
Final Evidence That
Marilyn Monroe Was Murdered

Most people throughout the world have read that Marilyn Monroe's death was caused by a drug overdose of Nembutals, the little yellow capsules whose street name is "yellowjackets," and whose generic name medically is sodium pentobarbital. This was the finding of the Suicide Investigation Team, who after giving their report to Coroner Thomas Curphey, announced it to an astonished press on August 18, 1962, less than two weeks after Marilyn's funeral.

Nembutal is classified as a sleeping compound and is manufactured by Abbott Laboratories in North Chicago, Illinois. This prescription drug comes in four forms: yellow capsules, colorless syrup, injectionable liquid, and suppository. Marilyn was taking the yellow capsules (1½ grain,) which were the strongest available in capsule form. She would only take a couple to get a good night's sleep. She knew her limitations. As case studies have proven in the past, with most individuals who rely on sleeping capsules there is a limit established by trial and error and the takers know their own capacity quite well.

Marilyn knew that two or three a night would be more than enough to produce the rest she required. The only side-effect would be lethargy the next morning. But after a cold shower and some hot black coffee, she would feel like tackling the world.

The fact remains that one of the doctors in the death bedroom that early morning of August 5, 1962, mentioned to Sergeant Jack Clemmons, that Marilyn had committed suicide by taking an overdose of Nembutal capsules, conveniently indicating an empty bottle which was said to have contained forty-seven or fifty Nembutals just the day before. The mistake is that the cause of death cannot be assumed just because a bottle of capsules has been emptied. However, the officer taking down the information for the police report wrote what the doctor had stated as the cause of death, and this became the "theme" passed on to the Suicide Investigation Team, who perpetuated that theme and delivered it to the news media as their finding.

Instead of her body being taken to the local funeral parlor and embalmed, destroying all evidence, the snag came when Deputy Coroner's Aide Lionel Grandison called the body to the coroner's ofice in downtown Los Angeles. We have to assume that if a body is autopsied, the process should reveal what the deceased took to commit suicide. The final answer was that no Nembutals were found in Marilyn's digestive system.

Had she taken all of those capsules orally, this would have produced two findings by Dr. Noguchi: (1) The yellow dye from the gel of the capsules would have stained the tissues of the digestive tract from the esophagus all the way down through the large and small intestines. (2) forty-seven or fifty capsules would leave a residue of more than half, either partially dissolved or completely undissolved, since a fatal dose is so much less than the amount it was reported that Marilyn consumed. However,

Dr. Noguchi found none of this to be true. There was no yellow stain, much less any trace of Nembutal capsules.

The blood, which is always examined first by the toxicologists, indicated a level of 4.5 mg. percent of "barbiturates" in the blood. According to medical authorities, a blood level of 3.3. mg. percent of Nembutal is lethal, even to a heavy user of the capsules. But the big mystery is this: if all of that lethal pentobarbital (Nembutal) was found in Marilyn's blood, why was there none found in her stomach contents? Since there was also no presence of the yellow stain, then just how did she get this drug into her system?

The obvious answer is agreed upon by most doctors who have reviewed this case: Marilyn received an overdose of pentobarbital by injection.

A slight controversy has always surrounded the yellow dye which stains the body tissues in the digestive tract. It seems that some authorities, who are not doctors by the way, just don't want to believe this fact. But it is very easy to prove and the first official place to start for me was Abbott Laboratories. Their spokesman personally stated as of the last week of September 1982 that Nembutal does have a yellow dye in the capsule and normally leaves a trace of yellow stain. If this company manufactures this product, then I felt confident that they would know the capabilities of their product.

But I decided to go one step further. I consulted the American Medical Association in New York and asked them for a firm answer on the question of whether Nembutal leaves a yellow stain in the digestive tract of a suicide victim who has ingested a quantity of same. Less than two hours later, the report came back. They had contacted Dr. George Hummer, a pathologist at St. Joseph's Hospital, who in turn had contacted Dr. Ronald Kornblaum, Chief Medical Examiner of the Los Angeles County Coroner's office. Their combined answers came back positive. Yes, Nembutal (in capsule form) does leave a yellow trace of the capsule gel in the mucous tissues.

Dr. Kornblaum even stated that when his office suspected a victim had overdosed on Nembutal, the first thing they looked for was the yellow stain. If this yellow stain is evident in the autopsy, the answer is usually Nembutal, the exception being some other lethal capsules with yellow dye. Similarly, if the tissues are red, the obvious answer is mostly Seconal, a red sleeping capsule with a red dye in the gel of the capsule that produces death in the same fashion as any other sleeping capsules when taken in excess.

The reader may think that I have belabored a point in taking all of this space to talk about the properties of a yellow capsule leaving a stain of the same color. This is why it is so important: In the case of Marilyn Monroe, where no such stain or even Nembutal capsules were found in her digestive system, it proves a very fundamental and vital point, damning all other evidence. This is that point: Since no yellow stain was found, there obviously were no Nembutal capsules ingested orally. Consider the fact that even the residue of her stomach, when examined under a polarized microscope that identifies all drugs known as "sleep-inducers" (including Nembutal), showed not a trace of any drug found in the stomach—only in the blood.

Conclusion: I discovered that even twenty years ago, when Marilyn died, the yellow dye would have been present, if she had really overdosed by swallowing the alleged Nembutals. No dye was found. I gave this new evidence to the district attorney's office in September 1982.

Yes, Marilyn Monroe did die of an overdose, but not by taking Nembutal orally. The fatal dosage was found only in her blood. The yellow dye was placed by the pharmaceutical manufacturer *only* in the capsule form; therefore, she had to be injected with the drug, yet no hypodermic needle was found in her house!

I conclude, based upon all the information and evidence secured during my intensive investigation, that Marilyn Monroe was murdered, and her murder was a massive cover-up.

More than twenty years have passed since Marilyn died. What follows is an update on many of those associated with her, both in life, and after her death.

XXIV

Cast of Characters—20 Years Later

I felt it might be interesting to the reader of this book to know what happened to those people associated with Marilyn Monroe during the last months of her life. Although our principal character, Marilyn Monroe, actually died the night of August 4, 1962, there are a great many survivors who were in her employ, her close friends, or persons that she associated with either personally or in her course of business.

President John F. Kennedy was assassinated in November, 1963, in Dallas, Texas. His brother Robert Kennedy, Senator from New York State, in June 1968, after celebrating primary victories in Idaho and California, was assassinated in the kitchen of the Ambassador Hotel in Los Angeles.

These three famous names, well known to the public, have passed out of the picture—but most of the persons listed below are still alive and can still be questioned under oath.

MRS. EUNICE MURRAY: Marilyn's companion-housekeeper, born March 3, 1902, in Chicago, Illinois. Her maiden name was Eunice Joerndt. On March 12, 1924, she married John Murray, described as a left-wing labor organizer. They built a home at 902 Franklin Street in Santa Monica, in the mid-'40s, and lived there until their divorce in 1949, at which time they sold the house to Mrs. Murray's friend, Dr. Ralph Greenson (Marilyn's psychiatrist). Dr. Greenson and Mrs. Murray were to remain friends over the years, and he was the one who recommended her to Marilyn Monroe as a companion-housekeeper ten months before Marilyn died.

Following Marilyn's death, Mrs. Murray took a trip to Europe, via Air France, leaving the United States on August 17, 1962, stating that she was going on a "pleasure trip" and would travel through France, Italy, Germany and Switzerland. Mrs. Murray continued to live in the Los Angeles area in the years since Marilyn's death, taking frequent vacations and trips, and enjoying a life of leisure. In the late 1970s, Mrs. Murray met and married a man from Bath, Maine, by the name of Blackmer. A few years later he died, and Mrs. Murray became the recipient of his estate. Up until September 1982, Mrs. Murray lived in an apartment in West Los Angeles, before moving most recently to live with her daughter in Santa Monica, California.

DR. RALPH ROMEO GREENSON: Marilyn's psychiatrist, resided at 902 Franklin Street, in the home built by Mrs. Murray and her husband. Dr. Greenson was born September 20, 1911, and died of congestive heart failure on November 24, 1979. He was born in New York, and his father was Joel O. Greenschpoon.

DR. HYMAN ENGELBERG: Marilyn's internist. He was born in 1911 and licensed to practice medicine in 1935. The bills he submitted to Probate Court for payment after Marilyn's death indicated that he had seen Marilyn twenty-seven times, during the period from June 28, 1962, to August 3, 1962, at which times he had given her various injections, which he has never explained.

A short time after Marilyn's death, Dr. Engelberg moved his offices from Wilshire Boulevard into the same building in Beverly Hills in which Dr. Greenson had his offices. It was Dr. Engelberg, in Marilyn's bedroom, that early morning of August 5, 1962, who officially pronounced her dead. It was also Dr. Engelberg, when asked what the cause of death might have been by Sergeant Jack Clemmons, who replied that Marilyn had consumed approximately fifty Nembutal capsules, and pointed to an empty bottle which had previously and allegedly contained Nembutal capsules.

He continues to practice in Beverly Hills as an internist who specializes in cardiac problems.

MARGOT PATRICIA NEWCOMB: She was press secretary for Marilyn Monroe, assigned to handle Marilyn's publicity by her employer, the Arthur Jacobs Agency. She was born on July 9, 1930, in Washington, D.C., the daughter of Carmen Adams Newcomb and the former Lillian Lee.

After Marilyn's funeral, Miss Newcomb flew to the Kennedy compound at Hyannisport, Massachusetts, where she stayed for a couple of weeks, before leaving the country and staying away for six months. During this period from August 1962 to February 1963, Miss Newcomb visited Germany, France, Holland, Denmark, Italy and Switzerland. She returned to the United States and landed a job in Washington on the government payroll as an information specialist in motion pictures for the United States Information Agency.

When Walter Winchell broke the news that Miss Newcomb was working in an office adjacent to that of Attorney General Bobby Kennedy, and had not properly filled out her civil service form, she was immediately dismissed, but then joined Bobby Kennedy's staff when he resigned his office as Attorney General of the United States to run for the office of Senator from New York State.

Later, when Pierre Salinger decided to run for senator in California, Miss Newcomb joined his campaign staff. In the early '70s, Miss Newcomb worked for a film production company in New York City by the name of Tomorrow Entertainment. Later she accepted a position in publicity for the Pickwick Public Relations Agency in New York City. In 1982, she took a publicity post in New York City with the offices of Rogers & Cowan, a company that she had worked for in previous years.

NORMAN JEFFRIES II: This is Mrs. Murray's son-in-law, who was employed by Marilyn as a "handyman." She reportedly paid him $180 per week, although the exact extent of his duties was never quite clear. It was Mrs. Murray who, after Dr. Greenson had broken one of the window panes in Marilyn's bedroom on the night of her death, called him in the middle of the night to repair the broken pane. This is quite an oddity in itself.

JOSEPH PAUL DiMAGGIO: The famous Yankee slugger was married to Marilyn Monroe in January 1954. His marriage to Marilyn was a stormy one, according to Marilyn, and it lasted for approximately eight months before she filed for divorce. DiMaggio now lives in San Francisco.

PETER LAWFORD: Lawford was married to the sister of the brothers Kennedy, Patricia Kennedy Lawford, and they lived in a luxurious beach house, north of the Santa Monica pier, on Pacific Coast Highway. Marilyn attended a few parties at this particular house, given by the Lawfords, at which

Bobby Kennedy was always present. After the assassination of President John F. Kennedy in Dallas, in November 1963, Patricia Kennedy Lawford sued her husband for divorce. Lawford stayed in Los Angeles, moving out of the plush beach house in Santa Monica, and remained somewhat active in the motion picture business. He had been a prominent member of the famous "Rat Pack" headed by Frank Sinatra, but in the ensuing years, for some unexplained reason, seemed to drop out of that group. For a brief period of time, Lawford met and married a much younger girl, but that too ended in divorce. In recent years, Lawford has not been a dominant character on the Hollywood scene.

PATRICIA KENNEDY LAWFORD: Mrs. Lawford, spent a great deal of her time during her marriage to the actor back in Hyannisport. She now lives in New York.

RALPH ROBERTS: A long-time friend of Marilyn, he was her personal masseur. He literally worshipped the ground she walked on, and she could always count on him as one of her very few close and trusted friends.

ALLAN (WHITEY) SNYDER: Whitey is a top make-up expert in the film industry, having made Marilyn up for her first screen test in 1947 at 20th Century-Fox Studios. Through the sixteen years that Marilyn was a star, Whitey was her sole make-up man.

A few years before Marilyn's death, she made a pact with Snyder: if she predeceased him in death, he would promise to make her up for her public, which he did at Westwood.

During the last ten years, he has been the head make-up man on the famous television series, "Little House On The Prairie."

JACK COLE: Cole, at Marilyn's request, was her dance choreographer for several of her films. Always a devoted friend, an expert in his profession, Jack Cole never believed that Marilyn committed suicide. Cole, who maintained residences both in New York City and Los Angeles, died in the middle-'70s.

LEE AND PAULA STRASBERG: When Marilyn moved to New York City, in November 1954, she became friends with the Strasbergs. They gave her theatrical instruction and coaching lessons, and proceeded to exert considerable influence over her. This led to Marilyn attending their acting school, known as the Actors Studio, in New York City.

Lee Strasberg went into acting, and appeared in a few major motion pictures. Paula died in the late seventies, Lee in 1982.

ARTHUR MILLER: Marilyn's former husband was not named in her will, and was not even in contact with her at the time of her death. He did not attend her funeral, although the coroner's office recorded that Miller was one of the first persons they called, even before DiMaggio, to ask if he would claim Marilyn's body from the morgue.

Today Miller has remarried, a younger girl who was a photographer, and continues to live in Connecticut.

DAVID CONOVER: Conover was the first professional photographer to capture Marilyn's likeness on film. During the ending of the war years, in early 1945, he was on assignment by *Stars and Stripes* Magazine to photograph pretty girls on the West Coast who were working in war plants and contributing to the war effort. It was Conover's pictures of Marilyn that appeared in *Stars and Stripes*, and eventually in a few of the men's magazines. At the time, she posed for *See, Titter, and Laugh,* which displayed a lot of legs and clevage, but no nudity. Conover was instrumental in Marilyn's becoming a model and leaving the war plant to join Emiline Sniveley's Blue Book Modeling Agency.

FRANK SINATRA: Marilyn had known him for a good many years. When she was at a low ebb in New York, after her divorce from Arthur Miller in the early part of 1961, Sinatra took Marilyn out frequently, even buying her the little while poodle which she named "Maf," and whose name was misspelled in most newspapers as "Mof." Actually it was an inside joke between her and the singer, because she had originally called the dog "Mafia," over Sinatra's objections, and then later she decided to shorten the name to "Maf."

TOM KELLEY: It was Tom Kelley and his wife who, back in 1948 at a time when Marilyn needed money, gave her $50 for posing one night on a sheet of red velvet in what was later to become the famous calendar picture. Kelley, who escalated Marilyn Monroe into the most famous nude in calendar history, still has his photography studio in West Hollywood. He is now semi-retired.

BOB SLATZER: Slatzer first met Marilyn when he was a newspaper reporter during the summer of 1946. Their relationship blossomed through the years over a sixteen-year period. During this time, he was her closest friend, confidante, and advisor, and in her early days as an actress even made up publicity releases which he sent out to enhance her image with the press.

Since Marilyn's death, he has meticulously pursued and ferreted out facts that were unknown and theretofore unpublished. He turned over his ten-year investigation in 1972 to Nick Harris Detectives for extensive investigation. Since that time, Slatzer was an executive at Columbia Pictures Corp., and has continued to write books and to direct and produce motion picture features and television series.

The preceding persons were those closely associated with Marilyn Monroe, at one time or another, during her life. Although they played a great part in Marilyn's life while she was living, there are those who played an equally important part in her destiny after she was found dead. They are:

SERGEANT JACK CLEMMONS: A veteran detective on the L.A.P.D., Clemmons was the Watch Commander at the West Los Angeles Police Station when he received word that Marilyn was dead.

Clemmons is now self-employed, selling swimming-pools, and resides in Reseda, California.

LIONEL GRANDISON: He was a deputy coroner's aide in 1962 and was coerced into signing Marilyn's death certificate, under pressure, and maintains to this day that she did not commit suicide.

He left the coroner's office and became a radio engineer. Grandison now produces radio and television programs.

DR. THEODORE CURPHEY: Dr. Curphey was Coroner of Los Angeles County when Marilyn Monroe died.

Today he is retired and living in Pasadena, California, and refuses to comment on Marilyn Monroe's death, only stating that the case was "properly handled" and that there is nothing to talk about twenty years later.

DR. THOMAS NOGUCHI: Best known as the "Coroner of the Stars." He performed the autopsy on Marilyn Monroe, who was his first "Star."

In the spring of 1982, Dr. Noguchi became the target of several accusations, including alleged wrongdoings in his administration and so-called unorthodox procedures in the coroner's office. As a result, Dr. Noguchi was relieved of his position, and an acting coroner was appointed. Dr. Noguchi remained on staff at the coroner's office but when the acting coroner decided that Dr. Noguchi was a bad influence, because certain sympathizers were causing conflict in the office management, Dr. Noguchi was transferred temporarily to the medical department at the University of Southern California. At the time of this writing, he is appealing his case to the civil service division.

JAMES HOFFA: Hoffa, a former President of the Teamsters Union, had no connection with Marilyn Monroe, except that he was using master wiretapper Bernard Spindel to set up wiretaps and various "bugs" wherever Bobby Kennedy spent time. Hoffa disappeared in 1975, and his body was never found.

BERNARD SPINDEL: Considered the master wiretapper of his time. He was retained by Hoffa to perform clandestine eavesdropping wherever Bobby Kennedy went. Spindel died February 2, 1972.

J. EDGAR HOOVER: As head of the F.B.I. for nearly four decades, Hoover left no stone unturned when it came to keeping track of the extramarital activities of Bobby and Jack Kennedy. In his files, which he kept quite meticulously, he had much classified information on both of the Kennedy brothers and their "romances" with various motion picture stars and other "ladies of the evening." Hoover died May 1, 1972.

Epilogue

The mystery of Marilyn Monroe's death has been persisting as a public outcry for the past twenty years. She has received more publicity in death than she ever gained during her illustrious career. Marilyn has far outclassed the legends that existed prior to her death of such luminaries as Rudolph Valentino, Clark Gable, and Jean Harlow. She has, since her death, become a legend of our time.

Although I never met Marilyn Monroe, after ten years investigating her death I feel I know more about Marilyn than most of the individuals who claim such "closeness" to Hollywood's Golden Girl. Recently, a television reporter asked me briefly to describe her. "She had charisma," I said. What more did I have to say?

After the twentieth anniversary of Marilyn's death, I was invited to appear on television programs throughout the United States and Canada. While in Detroit I appeared on the popular "Kelly and Company" TV show, with a live audience of 150 people. Just before the show aired, the producer asked for a show of hands from those who believed Marilyn had been murdered. I noticed about ten hands go up. After my interview, the same question was asked. This time nearly everyone was satisfied she did not commit suicide.

Each year the worldwide publicity speculating upon the unnatural causes of her death has changed the minds of many disbelievers. Now that you've read my book, I trust you formed an opinion; was it suicide, accidental death, or was it homicide?

I have contended for a decade she was murdered. So do many competent medical doctors, forensic pathologists, law enforcement officers and investigative reporters who have studied this case.

In September 1982 I provided the Los Angeles County District Attorney's office with the identification of the persons who I believe murdered Marilyn Monroe. I also gave them the identity of the sources said to have a tape recorded "bugged" "confession" of the killers. I had done my job, solving the most difficult case in my twenty three-year career.

On Saturday, October 23, 1982, at exactly 2:07 p.m., I officially closed case file number 72-4813, the investigation into the death of Marilyn Monroe. Among more than a million of our past assignments, this was the longest running case in the seventy-six-year history of my agency, Nick Harris Detectives, Inc.

Now it's up to the District Attorney and Grand Jury. Will they prosecute those persons responsible for her death, or will the death of Marilyn Monroe continue to remain a political cover-up?

Appendix

Marilyn wrote this letter while being held "prisoner" in an "insane asylum.""
From the collection of Robert Crivell, Published with permission.

Dear Lee & Paula,

     Dr. Kris has had me put
into the "New York Hospital - psichiatric division
under the care of two idiota doctors. They
both should not be my doctors.

     You haven't heard from me because
I'm locked up with all these poor
nutty people. I'm sure to end up a
nut if I stay in this nightmare. please
help me Lee, this is the last place I
should be - maybe if you called Dr. Kris
and assured her of my sensitivity and
that I must get back to class so
I'll be better prepared for "rain".

over

Dr, I try to remember what you
said once in class "that art goes far
beyond science"

And the same memories around
here I'd like to forget - like screaming
woman etc.

Please help me - if Dr. Kris
assures you I am all right - you
can assure her I am not.
I do not belong here!

I love you - both,

Marilyn

P.S. forgive the spelling - and there's nothing
to write on here. I'm on the dangerous floor
its like a cell. Can you imagine - cement blocks.
they put me in here because they lied to me
about calling my doctor & Joe and they had the
bathroom door locked so I broke the glass out.
side of that I haven't done anything that is uncooperative!

CENTRAL INTELLIGENCE AGENCY

WASHINGTON, D. C. 20505

PUBLIC AFFAIRS
Phone: (703) 351-7676

2 September 1982

Mr. Milo A. Speriglio
Nick Harris Detectives, Inc.
6740 Kester Avenue
Second Floor
Van Nuys, CA 91405

Dear Mr. Speriglio:

Thank you for writing Mr. Casey concerning the recent news coverage regarding the investigation of Marilyn Monroe's death. We appreciate the fact that you have gone on record stating that the Central Intelligence Agency was not involved in Marilyn Monroe's death. Actually, the CIA had nothing to do with her death and our Agency has vehemently denied such reports by the media.

We congratulate you on your excellent record as Director of the Nick Harris Detective Agency and encourage you to continue your good work.

Sincerely,

Alton D. Baxter, Jr.
Public Affairs Division

Part of F.B.I file on Marilyn Monroe—edited by F.B.I. prior to release.

FILE DESCRIPTION ~~ No 7/0 √ ?

SUBJECT _MARILYN MONROE_

FILE NOS. 62-31615 - 966, 967, 983
94 - 46406 - A
94 - 50672 - 5

~~VOLUME NO.~~ "SEE" REFERENCES

Office Mem **8***um* · UNIT ED STATES **8** GOVERNMENT

TO : L. V. Boardman

FROM : A. H. Belmont

SUBJECT: WALTER WINCHELL'S BROADCAST
July 1 , 1956

DATE: July 2, 1956

cc Mr. Nichols
cc Mr. Boardman
cc Mr. Belmont
cc Mr. Rosen
cc Mr. Branigan
cc Mr. Bland
cc Mr. Baumgardner
cc Mr. Cromer

Tolson
Nichols
Boardman
Belmont
Mason
Mohr
Parsons
Rosen
Tamm
Nease
Winterrowd
Tele. Room
Holloman
Gandy

Winchell's broadcast was not carried locally on station WTOP due to the broadcast of a baseball game. The following items of interest to the Bureau in Winchell's broadcast of above date were obtained from the New York Office.

WINCHELL SAID:

Playwright Arthur Miller, husband of Marilyn Monroe refused to disclose names of comrades with whom he once attended Red front meetings. Committee will astonish Miller by telling him those nine names.

COMMENT:

b7C

WINCHELL SAID:

International news; London - "Time and Tide " British publication, had a remarkable scoop. "Now that the cruel ways of Joe Stalin have been abandoned we hope that Mrs. Khrushchev will be released from Siberia. She was arrested and deported in 1938 by Stalin for whom Mr. Khruschev was carrying out mass purges.

COMMENT:

For information.

HC:alj

(9)

252

TO : Mr. L. V. Boardman   DATE: June 11, 1956

FROM : Mr. A. H. Belmont

cc - Mr. Nichols
     Mr. Boardman
     Mr. Belmont
     Mr. Rosen
     Mr. Branigan
     Mr. Bland
     Mr. Baumgardner
     Mr. Broden

SUBJECT: WALTER WINCHELL'S BROADCAST
         JUNE 10, 1956

WINCHELL SAID:

"Playwright Arthur Miller reported next husband of Marilyn
Monroe will get his marital freedom tomorrow. Next stop,_ - trouble.
The House Un-American Committee subpoena for Arthur Miller will check
into his entire inner circle, which also happens to be the inner
circle of Miss Monroe, all former communist sympathizers."

COMMENT:

b7C

WINCHELL SAID:

"Washington, D. C. The Senate investigators will stage
a very sensational melodrama on June 19, 1956, in New York City.
Six labor front leaders will be confronted by newspaperman Victor
Riesel, who lost his sight in the fight against labor racketeers."

COMMENT:

b7C

62-31615- 983

WINCHELL SAID:

"The next diplomatic bombshell for the west will be the
visit of Premier Nasser of Egypt to Yugoslavia and Marshal Tito. A

CWR:sm (9)

cc: Mr. Hitt

Date: August 19, 1955   40018   BY COURIER SERVICE

RECORDED - 86   105

To: Mr. Dennis A. Flinn   (Orig & 1)
       Director
EX-104 Office of Security
       Department of State
       515 22nd Street, N. W.
       Washington, D. C.

From: John Edgar Hoover, Director
       Federal Bureau of Investigation

Subject:

APPROPRIATE AGENCIES
AND FIELD OFFICES
ADVISED BY ROUTING
SLIP (S) OF
DATE 11-8-78

            The foregoing data are being furnished for your
information with the request that they not be further disseminated
in order to protect the identity of the informant in this case.

cc - 1 - Director   BY COURIER SERVICE
         Central Intelligence Agency   cc-1-Assistant Attorney General
         2430 E Street, N. W.   William F. Tompkins
         Washington, D. C.   (O-6 same date)

         Attention: Deputy Director, Plans

FVH:1um

58AUG 26 1955   SECRET

                  CONFIDENTIAL

                        254

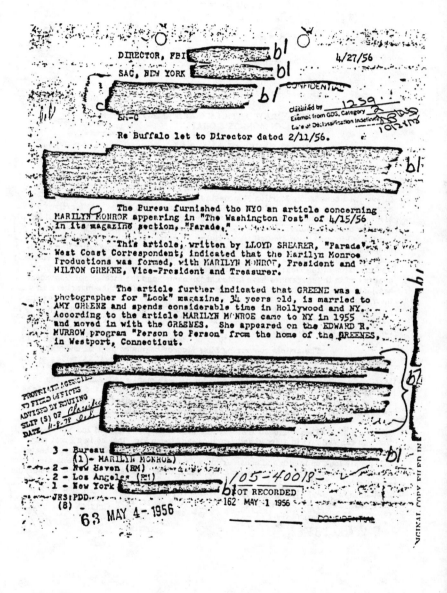

DIRECTOR, FBI [redacted] b1 4/27/56

SAC, NEW YORK [redacted] b1

[redacted] b1 ~~CONFIDENTIAL~~

Classified by 1259
Exempt from GDS, Category 2
Date of Declassification Indefinite

SM-C

Re Buffalo let to Director dated 2/11/56.

[redacted] b1

The Bureau furnished the NYO an article concerning MARILYN MONROE appearing in "The Washington Post" of 4/15/56 in its magazine section, "Parade."

This article, written by LLOYD SHEARER, "Parade" West Coast Correspondent, indicated that the Marilyn Monroe Productions was formed, with MARILYN MONROE, President and MILTON GREENE, Vice-President and Treasurer.

The article further indicated that GREENE was a photographer for "Look" magazine, 34 years old, is married to AMY GREENE and spends considerable time in Hollywood and NY. According to the article MARILYN MONROE came to NY in 1955 and moved in with the GREENES. She appeared on the EDWARD R. MURROW program "Person to Person" from the home of the GREENES, in Westport, Connecticut.

[redacted] b1

APPROPRIATE AGENCIES
AND FIELD OFFICES
ADVISED BY ROUTING
SLIP (S) OF Classified
DATE 11-8-78

3 - Bureau [redacted] b1
(1) - MARILYN MONROE)
2 - New Haven (RM)
2 - Los Angeles (RM)
1 - New York [redacted] b1

JHS:PDD
(8)

105-40018 -
NOT RECORDED
162 MAY 1 1956

63 MAY 4 - 1956

~~CONFIDENTIAL~~

ORIGINAL COPY FILED IN

TO : Mr. DeLoach   DATE: 7-9-63

FROM : M. A. Jones

SUBJECT: "PHOTOPLAY" ARTICLE CONCERNING
MARILYN MONROE'S DEATH

ALL INFORMATION CONTAINED
HEREIN IS UNCLASSIFIED

Walter Winchell's column in the July 8, 1963, issue of the "New York Mirror" contained the statement, "Photoplay's current article on the man who 'killed' Marilyn practically names him."

In accordance with your request, there follows a brief review of the information concerning Marilyn Monroe in the August, 1963, issue of "Photoplay", magazine. On page 10, a column by Winchell begins which states that Marilyn Monroe's death "and the married man responsible for it" was still getting considerable space in the foreign press. Winchell says the author of the articles, which are syndicated in papers on the Continent, claims he personally interviewed many people in Hollywood and New York who were aware of Miss Monroe's problems and claimed his sensational story was "big news." The "big news," according to Winchell, was the name of the "married man" involved. Winchell says "many of us" on the papers and in the magazines have hinted at the name, and the foreign correspondent has jumped to conclusions. Winchell says there is no proof that the married man was the villain, and many of Miss Monroe's friends now believe the overdose of sleeping pills was an accident. Winchell claims much of the foreign correspondent's story was recognized by him as having appeared in "Photoplay" and in the Hearst newspapers for which Winchell writes.

The article concerning Miss Monroe begins on page 52 under the caption, "One Year Later Marilyn Monroe's Killer Still At Large!" A review of this article reveals Winchell's claim that it practically names the man who "killed" Marilyn is nothing more than a plug for a cheap magazine. Actually, the article comes noway near identifying anyone. The only "clues" to the identity of the alleged married man who had an affair with Marilyn and "caused" her suicide when he rejected her could apply to any number of prominent individuals.

These "clues" are: that the man is happily married and has children; that you can see him in a crowd and reach out and touch him; that he is a great man, famous, known the world over; that he can be seen on television and in movie theaters; that people look up to him and consider his wife and children lucky; that he is mentioned almost daily in newspapers and magazines; and that he is considered a "truly honorable man."

Enclosure
DWB:car
(4)

ENCLOSURE

PHOTO BEHIND FILE

7 2 AUG 13 1963

REC 31   105-40018-4

ST-104

AUG 6 1963

ALL INFORMATION CONTAINED
HEREIN IS UNCLASSIFIED
EXCEPT WHERE SHOWN
OTHERWISE

M. A. Jones to DeLoach memo
RE: "PHOTOPLAY" ARTICLE CONCERNING MARILYN MONROE'S DEATH

The article alleges the affair between this man and Miss Monroe began during the "worst time of her life and the best time of his." The alleged man was celebrating his good fortune in reaching a height in his career "he never before dreamed" would be possible. The remainder of the article allegedly outlines the end of the romance and Miss Monroe's final efforts to renew the relationship. The article states that she telephoned the man on Sunday night, August 5, 1962, and when he said he would not leave his wife and could not see Miss Monroe "any more," she swallowed a "handful" of sleeping pills. The article claims she later called the man again, implying that she told him of having taken the pills, only to have him hang up on her and states that the last sound she heard was the "buzzing of the receiver in her hand." after the man broke the telephone connection.

The article states that Miss Monroe's housekeeper has "vanished" and that her publicity agent, Pat Newcombe, is now working in Washington, D. C. It says her second husband, Joe DiMaggio, is the only one who remains faithful and that the man who killed Miss Monroe is still at large and can never be arrested. But, the article asserts, "Wherever he goes, whatever he touches, whomever he sees; he thinks of Marilyn. His guilt never leaves him, his fear has become his friend."

RECOMMENDATION:

For information.

257

Mr. E. S. Miller

T. J. Smith

1 - Mr. He?ngton (Press Office)
1 - Mr. T. J. Smith
1 - Mr. Sizoo

7/23/73

ALL INFORMATION CO
HEREIN IS UNCLASSI
EX????
O??????SE

NORMAN MAILER
INFORMATION CONCERNING

To advise of speculation concerning FBI complicity in the death of Marilyn Monroe propounded by author Norman Mailer in his soon-to-be-published biography of the deceased actress.

"Marilyn," a 270-page biography (New York; Grosset and Dunlap,) priced at $19.95, is scheduled for publication on 8/1/73. It reportedly has a first American printing of 285,000 copies and is the August selection of the Book-of-the-Month Club.

Following Miss Monroe's death by drug overdose in 1962, there was a spate of rumors, originating on the West Coast alleging she was having an affair with the then Attorney General Robert F. Kennedy, and that her death was in some way related to this and/or was the result of a plot revolving around some of her associates who allegedly had past Communist Party affiliations or sympathies. These rumors were embellished upon at that time in various sensational-type gossip magazines and in a short book published in July, 1964, entitled "The Strange Death of Marilyn Monr" by Frank A. Capell. These allegations were branded false and no factual support existed for them.

Mailer, in his new book, has repeated some of these same rumors and has given them a bizarre twist.

As to whether Miss Monroe took her own life, Mailer answers "possibly" - and then suggests other possibilities. One of these is the suggestion that the FBI, CIA or the Mafia found it of interest that Robert Kennedy, brother of the President John Ken was reputed to be having an affair with the movie star. Mailer suggests that "right-wing" FBI and CIA Agents had a "huge motiva to murder Marilyn Monroe in order to embarrass the Kennedy fam

1 - 100-370923 (Norman Mailer)
1 - 105-40018 (Marilyn Monroe)

RPF:rlc
(6)

5AUG 7 1973

105-40018-

NOT RECORDED

152 AUG 1 1973

CONTINUED - OVER

258

Memorandum to Mr. E. S. Miller
Re: Norman Mailer

claiming the FBI and CIA were furious with the Kennedys because
following the Bay of Pigs invasion President Kennedy was moving to
limit the power of these agencies.

Mailer has admitted in recent press interviews concerning
his book that he has no evidence to support his theory and that it is
based on his "writer's instinct" and on speculation.

A second allegation purportedly contained in the book was
recently brought to the attention of the Los Angeles Office by Lloyd
Shearer, editor of Parade Magazine. This allegation is that in 1962
FBI Agents in Los Angeles went to the telephone company in Santa Monica,
California, and removed a "paper tape" of Marilyn Monroe's telephone
calls, some of which according to Mailer, were presumably to the
White House or White House staff on the night of her death.

This is false and neither the files of the Los Angeles Office
nor FBI Headquarters indicate the existence of any such tapes. This
again appears to be a variation of a spurious charge contained in Capell's
1964 book in which he alleged that such tapes were in the custody of
the Los Angeles Police Department.

Norman Mailer is an eccentric but well-known author, who
in the past has won a Pulitzer Prize and a National Book Award. He
is the author of "The Naked and the Dead," "The Deer Park," "An
American Dream," "Cannibals and Christians," "The Armies of the
Night," and "Miami and the Siege of Chicago."

b6

259

STATE FILE NUMBER

LOCAL REGISTRATION DISTRICT AND CERTIFICATE NUMBER 7053 17716

CERTIFICATE OF DEATH
STATE OF CALIFORNIA—DEPARTMENT OF PUBLIC HEALTH

1a NAME OF DECEASED—FIRST NAME	1b MIDDLE NAME	1c LAST NAME	2a DATE OF DEATH—MONTH DAY YEAR	2b HOUR
Marilyn		Monroe	August 5, 1962	3:40 a.

3 SEX	4 COLOR OR RACE	5 BIRTHPLACE (STATE OR FOREIGN COUNTRY)	6 DATE OF BIRTH	7 AGE	IF UNDER 1 YEAR	IF UNDER 24 HOURS
Female	Cauc.	Los Angeles, Calif.	June 1, 1926	36		

8 NAME AND BIRTHPLACE OF FATHER	9 MAIDEN NAME AND BIRTHPLACE OF MOTHER	10 CITIZEN OF WHAT COUNTRY	11 SOCIAL SECURITY NUMBER
unk unk	Gladys Pearl Baker —Mexico	United States	563-32-0764

12 LAST OCCUPATION	13 NUMBER OF YEARS IN SERVICE	14 NAME OF LAST EMPLOYING COMPANY OR FIRM	15 KIND OF INDUSTRY OR BUSINESS
Actress	20	20th Century-Fox	Motion Pictures

16 MARRIED, NEVER MARRIED, WIDOWED, DIVORCED	17 SPECIFY MARRIED OR OTHER	18a NAME OF PRESENT SPOUSE	18b PRESENT OR LAST OCCUPATION OF SPOUSE
none	Divorced		

19a PLACE OF DEATH—NAME OF HOSPITAL	19b STREET ADDRESS		
	12305 -5th Helena Drive		

19c CITY OR TOWN	19d COUNTY	19e LENGTH OF STAY IN COUNTY OF DEATH	19f LENGTH OF STAY IN CALIFORNIA
Los Angeles	Los Angeles	36	36

20a LAST USUAL RESIDENCE—STREET ADDRESS	20b INSIDE CITY CORPORATE LIMITS	21a NAME OF INFORMANT (OTHER THAN SPOUSE)
12305 -5th Helena Drive		Mrs. Inez C. Melson

20c CITY OR TOWN	20d COUNTY	20e STATE	21b ADDRESS OF INFORMANT
Los Angeles	Los Angeles	Calif.	9110 Sunset Blvd.

22a PHYSICIAN'S OR CORONER'S CERTIFICATION	22b PHYSICIAN OR CORONER SIGNATURE
autopsy	By Theo. J. Curphey M D, Coroner Deputy
	22c ADDRESS HALL OF JUSTICE LOS ANGELES 22d DATE SIGNED 8-28-62

23	24a DATE	25 NAME OF CEMETERY OR CREMATORY	26 EMBALMER SIGNATURE
Entombment	Aug. 8, 1962	Westwood Memorial Park	Clarence Whyte M.D.

27 NAME OF FUNERAL DIRECTOR	28 DATE RECEIVED BY LOCAL REGISTRAR	29 LOCAL REGISTRAR SIGNATURE
Westwood Village Mortuary	Sep 12 '62	Joann M. Vol.

30 CAUSE OF DEATH	PART I. DEATH WAS CAUSED BY: IMMEDIATE CAUSE (a)	ACUTE BARBITURATE POISONING	APPROXIMATE INTERVAL BETWEEN ONSET AND DEATH
	CONDITIONS, IF ANY, WHICH GAVE RISE TO ABOVE CAUSE DUE TO (b)	INGESTION OF OVERDOSE	
	DUE TO (c)		
PART II. OTHER SIGNIFICANT CONDITIONS CONTRIBUTING TO DEATH BUT NOT RELATED TO THE TERMINAL DISEASE CONDITION GIVEN IN PART I (a)			

31 OPERATION—CHECK ONE	32 DATE OF OPERATION	33 AUTOPSY—CHECK ONE
		X

34a SPECIFY ACCIDENT SUICIDE OR HOMICIDE	34b DESCRIBE HOW INJURY OCCURRED
Probable Suicide	As Above

35a TIME OF INJURY HOUR	34 DATE	35b INJURY OCCURRED	35c PLACE OF INJURY	35d CITY TOWN OR LOCATION	COUNTY	STATE
3:40 a.	8-5-62	WHILE AT WORK / NOT WHILE AT WORK	Home	Los Angeles	L.A.	Calif

This is a true certified copy of the record if it bears the seal of the County Recorder imprinted in purple ink.

FEE $2.00   SEP 24 1964

Ray E. Lee COUNTY RECORDER
AND DEPUTY COUNTY ASSESSOR OFFICER
LOS ANGELES COUNTY, CALIFORNIA

COUNTY RECORDER LOS ANGELES COUNTY · CALIFORNIA

260

COUNTY OF LOS ANGELES
OFFICE OF CORONER
BODY FULL LENGTH ANTERIOR

NAME *Marilyn Monroe*   Date *8/5/62*   File # *81128*

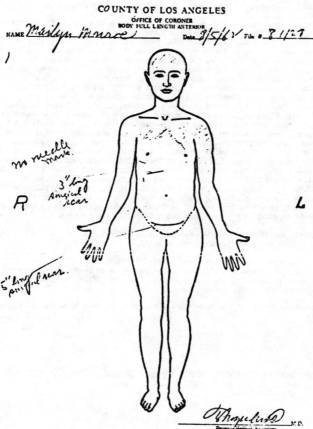

no needle mark.

R

3" long surgical scar.

L

5" long surgical scar.

_____ M.D.
Deputy Medical Examiner.

261

Re Death Report of Marilyn Monroe — L.A. Police Dpt.

Death was pronounced on 8/5/62 at 3:45 A.M., Possible Accidental, having taken place between the times of 8/4 and 8/5/62, 3:35 A.M. at residence located at 12305 Fifth Helena Drive, Brentwood, in Rptg. Dist. 314, Report # 62-509 463.

Marilyn Monroe on August 4, 1962 retired to her bedroom at about eight o'clock in the evening; Mrs. Eunice Murray of 933 Ocean Ave., Santa Monica, Calif., 395-7752, 61390, noted a light in Miss Monroe's bedroom. Mrs. Murray was not able to arouse Miss Monroe when she went to the door, and when she tried the door again at 3:30 A.M. when she noted the light still on, she found it to be locked. Thereupon Mrs. Murray observed Miss Monroe through the bedroom window and found her lying on her stomach in the bed and the appearance seemed unnatural. Mrs. Murray then called Miss Monroe's psychiatrist, Dr. Ralph R. Greenson of 436 North Roxbury Drive, Beverly Hills, Calif, CR 14050. Upon entering after breaking the bedroom window, he found Miss Monroe possibly dead. Then he telephoned Dr. Hyman Engelberg of 9730 Wilshire Boulevard, also of Beverly Hills, CR 54366, who came over and then pronounced Miss Monroe dead at 3:35 A.M. Miss Monroe was seen by Dr. Greenson on August 4, 1962 at 5:15 P.M., at her request, because she was not able to sleep. She was being treated by him for about a year. She was nude when Dr. Greenson found her dead with the telephone receiver in one hand and lying on her stomach. The Police Department was called and when they arrived they found Miss Monroe in the condition described above, except for the telephone which was removed by Dr. Greenson. There were found to be 15 bottles of medication on the night table and some were prescription. A bottle marked 1½ grains Nembutal, prescription #20853 and prescribed by Dr. Engelberg, and referring to this particular bottle, Dr. Engelberg made the statement that he prescribed a refill for this about two days ago and he further stated there probably should have been about 50 capsules at the time this was refilled by the pharmacist.

Description of Deceased: Female Caucasian, age 36, height 5.4, weight 115 pounds, blonde hair, blue eyes, and slender, medium build.

Occupation: Actress, Probable cause of death: overdose of nembutal, body discovered 8/5/62 at 3:25 A.M. Taken to County Morgue — from there to Westwood Mortuary. Report made by Sgt. R. E. Byron, #2730, W. L.A. Detective Division. Next of kin: Gladys Baker (Mother).

Coroner's office notified. The body was removed from premises by Westwood Village Mortuary.

(8/5/62 11 AM LA hf - J. R. Brukles 5629)

First police report released by Sargeant Jack Clemmons.

FOLLOW-UP REPORT

☐ MULTIPLE REPORT   DR 62-509 463

TYPE CRIME	ADDITIONAL MAJOR CRIMES COMMITTED—THIS INCIDENT		
DEATH REPORT	"FILE"		

DATE AND TIME OCCURRED	DATE AND TIME OF THIS REPORT	LOCATION OF OCCURRENCE	RPTG. DIST.
8-4/5-62 8P/3:35A	8-6-62 4:15P	12305 Fifth Helena Dr.	814

VICTIM'S NAME (as listed on orig. report)	LIC NO INVOLVED VEHICLE	CONNECTING PROPERTY REPORTS
MONROE, Marilyn		

Property Recovery		TOTAL	PARTIAL	NONE	Additional Property	LOSS	THIS REPORT	$
Property Disposition		BOOKED	RELEASED BY DEPT			RECOVERY		$

Case Status	REPORT UNFOUNDED	CLEARED	☐	RECLASSIFY TO.		MAINTAIN WANTS	YES
	COMPLAINT REFUSED	☒ INVEST CONT				IN PROPERTY FILE?	NO

PERSON(S) ARRESTED	LA OR JS NO.	SEX	DESC	AGE	HGT.	WGT.	HAIR	EYES	NTA DATE	CHARGE	CRT. DIV.

(1) EXPLAIN INVESTIGATION PROGRESS AND STATUS. (2) DESCRIBE ANY CHANGE IN M.O. (3) WHEN VICTIM AND/OR WITNESSES LISTED IN CRIME REPORT HAVE NOT BEEN INTERVIEWED, GIVE REASON. (4) IF ADDITIONAL PROPERTY LOSS INVOLVED, ITEMIZE, DESCRIBE AND SHOW VALUE, LISTING ALL SERIAL NUMBERS. IF PARTIAL RECOVERY, LIST PROPERTY RECOVERED, USING ITEM NUMBER, DESCRIPTION (SERIAL NO., MONOGRAMS, ETC.) AND VALUE AS IT APPEARS ON INITIAL REPORT. EXPLAIN ANY CHANGES FOUND NECESSARY IN PROPERTY DESCRIPTIONS REPORT ALL SERIAL NUMBERS AND INSCRIPTIONS DEVELOPED DURING INVESTIGATION.

ITEM NO	PERSON REPORTING OR ADDITIONAL PERSONS INTERVIEWED	RESIDENCE ADDRESS	CITY	RESIDENCE PHONE	BUSINESS PHONE

Upon reinterviewing both Dr. Ralph R. Greenson (Wit #1 and Dr. Hyman Engelberg (Wit #2) they both agree to the following time sequence of their actions.

Dr. Greenson received a phone call from Mrs Murray (reporting person) at 3:30A, 8-5-62 stating that she was unable to get into Miss Monroe's bedroom and the light was on. He told her to pound on the door and look in the window and call him back. At 3:35A, Mrs Murray called back and stated Miss Monroe was laying on the bed with the phone in her hand and looked strange. Dr. Greenson was dressed by this time, left for deceased residence which is about one mile away. He also told Mrs Murray to call Dr. Engelberg.

Dr. Greenson arrived at deceased house at about 3:40A. He broke the window pane and entered through the window and removed the phone from her hand.

Rigor Mortis had set in. At 3:50A, Dr. Engelberg arrived and pronounced Miss Monroe dead. The two doctors talked for a few moments. They both believe that it was about 4A when Dr. Engelberg called the Police Department.

A check with the Complaint Board and WLA Desk, indicates that the call was received at 4:25A. Miss Monroe's phone, GR 61890 has been checked and no toll calls were made during the hours of this occurrence Phone number 472-4830 is being checked at the present time.

R.E. Byron 2730

DATE AND TIME TYPED	DIVISION	CLERK	INTERVIEWING OFFICER(S)	SER. NO.	DIVISION	PERSON REPORTING (SIGNATURE)		
8-6-62 10:25A WLA D MS			R E BYRON 2730 WLA D			X	R C NO	DATE IS B.C. NO.

Second police report released by Sargeant R.E. Byron.

OFFICE OF COUNTY CORONER

Date __Aug. 5, 1962__   Time __10:30 a.m.__

I performed an autopsy on the body of   MARILYN MONROE

at the Los Angeles County Coroner's Mortuary, Hall of Justice, Los Angeles,

and from the anatomic findings and pertinent history I ascribe the death to:

           ACUTE BARBITURATE POISONING

DUE TO: INGESTION OF OVERDOSE

                                    (final 8/27/62)

ANATOMICAL SUMMARY

EXTERNAL EXAMINATION:

1. Lavidity of face and chest with
   slight ecchymosis of the left side
   of the back and left hip.

2. Surgical scar, right upper quadrant
   of the abdomen.

3. Suprapubic surgical scar.

RESPIRATORY SYSTEM:

1. Pulmonary congestion and minimal
   edema.

LIVER AND BILIARY SYSTEM:

1. Surgical absence of gallbladder.

2. Acute passive congestion of liver.

UROGENITAL SYSTEM:

1. Congestion of kidneys.

DIGESTIVE SYSTEM:

1. Marked congestion of stomach with
   petechial mucosal hemorrhage.

2. Absence of appendix.

3. Congestion and purplish discoloration
   of the colon.

EXTERNAL EXAMINATION:

The unembalmed body is that of a 36-year-old
well-developed, well-nourished Caucasian
female weighing 117 pounds and measuring
65½ inches in length. The scalp is covered
with bleached blond hair. The eyes are
blue. The fixed lividity is noted in the
face, neck, chest, upper portions of arms
and the right side of the abdomen. The
faint lividity which disappears upon pressure
is noted in the back and posterior aspect
of the arms and legs. A slight ecchymotic
area is noted in the left hip and left side
of lower back. The breast shows no significant lesion. There is a horizontal 3-inch
long surgical scar in the right upper
quadrant of the abdomen. A suprapubic
surgical scar measuring 5 inches in length
is noted.

The conjunctivae are markedly congested;
however, no ecchymosis or petechiae are
noted. The nose shows no evidence of
fracture. The external auditory canals
are not remarkable. No evidence of trauma
is noted in the scalp, forehead, cheeks,
lips or chin. The neck shows no evidence
of trauma. Examination of the hands and
nails shows no defects. The lower extremities show no evidence of trauma.

BODY CAVITY:

The usual Y-shaped incision is made to
open the thoracic and abdominal cavities
The pleural and abdominal cavities contain

3

no excess of fluid or blood. The mediastinum
shows no shifting or widening. The diaphragm
is within normal limits. The lower edge
of the liver is within the costal margin.
The organs are in normal position and
relationship.

CARDIOVASCULAR SYSTEM:

The heart weighs 300 grams. The pericardial
cavity contains no excess of fluid. The
epicardium and pericardium are smooth and
glistening. The left ventricular wall
measures 1.1 cm. and the right 0.2 cm.
The papillary muscles are not hypertrophic.
The chordae tendineae are not thickened or
shortened. The valves have the usual number
of leaflets which are thin and pliable.
The tricuspid valve measures 10 cm., the
pulmonary valve 6.5 cm., mitral valve 9.5
cm. and aortic valve 7 cm. in circumference.
There is no septal defect. The foramen
ovale is closed.

The coronary arteries arise from their usual
location and are distributed in normal
fashion. Multiple sections of the anterior
descending branch of the left coronary artery
with a 5 mm. interval demonstrate a patent
lumen throughout. The circumflex branch
and the right coronary artery also demonstrate
a patent lumen. The pulmonary artery contains
no thrombus.

The aorta has a bright yellow smooth intima.
RESPIRATORY SYSTEM:

The right lung weighs 465 grams and the left
420 grams. Both lungs are moderately congested
with some edema. The surface is dark red
with mottling. The posterior portion of the
lungs shows severe congestion. The tracheo-
bronchial tree contains no aspirated material
or blood. Multiple sections of the lungs

266

show congestion and edematous fluid exuding
from the cut surface. No consolidation or
suppuration is noted. The mucosa of the
larynx is grayish white.

LIVER AND BILIARY SYSTEM:

The liver weighs 1890 grams. The surface
is dark brown and smooth. There are marked
adhesions through the omentum and abdominal
wall in the lower portion of the liver as
the gallbladder has been removed. The
common duct is widely patent. No calculus
or obstructive material is found. Multiple
sections of the liver show slight accentuation
of the lobular pattern; however, no hemorrhage
or tumor is found.

HEMIC AND LYMPHATIC SYSTEM:

The spleen weighs 190 grams. The surface
is dark red and smooth. Section shows dark
red homogeneous firm cut surface. The
malpighian bodies are not clearly identified.
There is no evidence of lymphadenopathy.
The bone marrow is dark red in color.

ENDOCRINE SYSTEM:

The adrenal glands have the usual architec-
tural cortex and medulla. The thyroid glands
are of normal size, color and consistency.

URINARY SYSTEM:

The kidneys together weigh 350 grams. Their
capsules can be stripped without difficulty.
Dissection shows a moderately congested
parenchyma. The cortical surface is smooth.
The pelves and ureters are not dilated or
stenosed. The urinary bladder contains
approximately 150 cc. of clear straw-colored
fluid. The mucosa is not altered.

5

GENITAL SYSTEM:

The external genitalia shows no gross
abnormality. Distribution of the pubic
hair is of female pattern. The uterus
is of the usual size. Multiple sections
of the uterus show the usual thickness of
the uterine wall without tumor nodules.
The endometrium is grayish yellow, measuring
up to 0.2 cm in thickness. No polyp or
tumor is found. The cervix is clear,
showing no nabothian cysts. The tubes are
intact. The openings of the fimbria are
patent. The right ovary demonstrates
recent corpus luteum hæmorrhagicum. The
left ovary shows corpora lutea and albicantia.
A vaginal smear is taken.

DIGESTIVE SYSTEM:

The esophagus has a longitudinal folding
mucosa. The stomach is almost completely
empty. The contents is brownish mucoid
fluid. The volume is estimated to be no
more than 20 cc. No residue of the pills
is noted. A smear made from the gastric
contents and examined under the polarized
microscope shows no refractile crystals.
The mucosa shows marked congestion and
submucosal petechial hemorrhage diffusely.
The duodenum shows no ulcer. The contents
of the duodenum is also examined under
polarized microscope and shows no refractile
crystals. The remainder of the small
intestine shows no gross abnormality. The
appendix is absent. The colon shows
marked congestion and purplish discoloration.
The fecal contents is light brown and formed.
The mucosa shows no discoloration.

The pancreas has a tan lobular architecture.
Multiple sections shows a patent duct.

SKELETOMUSCULAR SYSTEM:

The clavicle, ribs, vertebrae and pelvic
bones show no fracture lines. All bones
of the extremities are examined by palpation
showing no evidence of fracture.

HEAD AND CENTRAL NERVOUS SYSTEM:

The brain weighs 1440 grams. Upon reflection
of the scalp there is no evidence of contusion
or hemorrhage. The temporal muscles are
intact. Upon removal of the dura mater the
cerebrospinal fluid is clear. The super-
ficial vessels are slightly congested. The
convolutions of the brain are not flattened.
The contour of the brain is not distorted.
No blood is found in the epidural, subdural
or subarachnoid spaces. Multiple sections
of the brain show the usual symmetrical
ventricles and basal ganglia. Examination
of the cerebellum and brain stem shows no
gross abnormality. Following removal of
the dura mater from the base of the skull
and calvarium no skull fracture is demonstrated.

Liver temperature taken at 10:30 a. m.
registered 89° F.

SPECIMEN:

Unembalmed blood is taken for alcohol and
barbiturate examination. Liver, kidney,
stomach and contents, urine and intestine
are saved for further toxicological study.
A vaginal smear is made.

T. NOGUCHI, M. D.
DEPUTY MEDICAL EXAMINER

TN:ag:G
8-13-62